THE
STRATEGY
OF
EXECUTION

THE
STRATEGY
OF
EXECUTION

THE FIVE-STEP GUIDE FOR TURNING VISION INTO ACTION

LIZ MELLON
AND
SIMON CARTER

New York   Chicago   San Francisco   Athens   London   Madrid
Mexico City   Milan   New Delhi   Singapore   Sydney   Toronto

1 2 3 4 5 6 7 8 9 0   DOC/DOC   1 8 7 6 5 4 3

ISBN   978-0-07-181531-4
MHID   0-07-181531-7

e-ISBN   978-0-07-181532-1
e-MHID   0-07-181532-5

Library of Congress Cataloging-in-Publication Data
Mellon, Elizabeth.
  The strategy of execution : a five step guide for turning vision into action / Liz Mellon and Simon Carter.
    pages cm
  ISBN 978-0-07-181531-4 (alk. paper)—ISBN 0-07-181531-7 (alk. paper)
1. Strategic planning. 2. Management. I. Title.
  HD30.28.M445 2014
  658.4'012—dc23

                                                        2013032406

McGraw-Hill Education books are available at special quantity discounts to use as premiums and sales promotions, or for use in corporate training programs. To contact a representative, please visit the Contact Us page at www.mhprofessional.com.

Dedication

To love, lost and found

Contents

Acknowledgments

We are grateful to many people who have helped us. Our first thanks must go to the (literally) thousands of executives who have shared with us their hopes and fears in conversations spanning 30 years. Their passion and energy about executing strategy have ignited our own.

We interviewed a variety of people, from Olympic athletes and diplomats to CEOs, some of whom agreed to be quoted here. Irene Dorner, the president and CEO of HSBC America, has given us ideas as well as a couple of leadership laws (such as the Dorner Law of Unintended Outcomes). David Levin, Tom Albanese, Jeremy Pelczer, Dominique Fournier, Nick Forster, and Pramod Bhasin all shared their own hard-won experiences of strategy execution as CEOs. Sir Jeremy Greenstock helped us to understand parallels between business and the heady diplomatic heights of the UN in New York. Ali Gill combined her Olympic prowess with psychological insight to tackle the challenges of leading change with self-insight. Rob Kaiser shared details from his large database on the skills of strategy compared with execution capabilities. Gareth Kaminski-Cook, Karina Robinson, Philippa Rodriguez, Thomas Kochs, Greg Marchi, Ronnie Bootle, Jack Krellé, Mark Selby, Jenny Duvalier, Claudia Bidwell, and Tony O'Driscoll shared theirs and others' stories of taking ownership and getting stuff done. Stuart Crainer and Des Dearlove, the midwives of ideas, took time off from running Thinkers 50 to help us straighten out our thoughts. And last but not least, the ever-generous Tim Jenkins followed his photo shoot with Mick Jagger to capture us for this book.

Our heartfelt thanks to all those named and not named here.

Foreword

by Costas Markides, Robert P. Bauman Chair in Strategic Leadership; Professor
of Strategy and Entrepreneurship, London Business School

Today more than ever, strategy has to involve people—both at a rational and an emotional level. Unless companies find ways to engage their people's energies and passion in developing new strategic ideas as well as putting these ideas into action, their strategy—however brilliant—will fail. This idea is at the heart of *The Strategy of Execution,* and Liz Mellon and Simon Carter have done an admirable job in putting together an impressive list of ideas and tactics on how companies could achieve such a lofty goal.

Psychologists will tell us that to win people's minds and hearts for anything, we must take them through four stages: In the first stage, you must communicate what you are trying to sell to them (i.e., our strategy) so that people start saying: "Yes, I know what our strategy is." In stage two, you must explain *why* you have decided on this particular strategy. By the end of this stage, you want your people to be saying: "I know what our strategy is and I understand why we have decided to undertake this particular strategy. I also understand why this strategy is important *for me.*"

In stage three, you need to make the strategy believable to people. You need to make them feel that the strategy is achievable so that by the end of this stage they say: "I know what the strategy is, I understand why it's important and, you know, I think I can do this. It's not an impossible thing." Finally, in stage four you really have to make the whole thing emotional so that employees start saying: "I know what the strategy is, I understand why we need it and I will *personally* contribute to its successful implementation." This is emotional commitment and as Mellon and Carter argue in their book, this is what makes or breaks a strategy.

Lack of emotional commitment toward strategy is certainly a key obstacle to its successful implementation. The book offers a wealth of ideas on how to achieve this emotional commitment not only from top executives—the Village Elders and the top 100 executives that make up the Village—but also and more importantly from every employee in the organization. But sprinkled in the book are also ideas on how to overcome two other major obstacles to successful execution of one's strategy.

The first obstacle is *lack of clarity*. By this I mean that the majority of employees do not even know what their company's strategy is. It's hard to implement something if you don't know what it is you are implementing! The question, therefore, that arises is "why is it that most employees do not know their company's strategy?"

A possible reason may be that top management has failed to communicate clearly and convincingly what their strategy is. But in my opinion, communication is not the real culprit. More often than not, what top management communicates again and again is not strategy but "motherhood and apple pie" statements that they call "strategy." These fail to provide the necessary direction that employees crave for.

Strategy is not a goal or an objective—it is simply the difficult choices that the organisation has made on three dimensions: the customers we will focus on and the customers we will *not*; the products we will offer and the ones we will *not*; the activities we will perform and the ones we will *not*. What gives clarity to people is stating clearly and explicitly what you are *not* going to do rather than what you will. Making these choices is extremely difficult because at the time of choice, nobody knows for sure what the correct decision is. As a result, most companies shy away from making the difficult calls necessary. Instead, they come up with meaningless statements like "Our strategy is to be the preferred supplier to our customers" or "Our strategy is to be number 1." No wonder that employees do not know what they need to do to execute strategy. This is why this book's recommendation that leaders need to focus on no more than five strategic initiatives is so important.

The second obstacle to execution is a *poor fit between the strategy and the company's "Organizational Environment."* If there is one thing we have learned after 50 years of research in social psychology, it is that much more than we'd like to believe, the "environment" in which we operate determines how we behave. As a result, if we want our employees to behave in ways that support (as opposed to hinder) the execution of our strategy, we must first put in place the "right" Organizational Environment.

This implies that a company that wants its strategy to be implemented properly must first ask the question "What Organizational Environment must I create internally to elicit the employee behaviours that will support my chosen strategy?" The Organizational Environment of any company is made up of four key ingredients: the measurement and incentive systems of the firm; its culture, values and norms; its structure and processes; and its people, including their skills, mindsets and attitudes. Without first putting in place an appropriate environment, the strategy will almost certainly fail.

I cannot emphasize this point strongly enough. Company after company send their executives on courses to help them change their attitudes and behaviors, to make them more innovative or more customer-oriented or whatever. What they forget is that training does not change people's attitudes or behaviors. People will not change what they do because we tell them to. They will only change if we put in place the right incentives and the right culture and values—in short, the right Organizational Environment. Again, the book provides numerous ideas on how to do this.

Not only does the book offer specific ideas on how to execute today's strategy but it also covers the issue of execution *over time*. As we all know, no strategy will remain unique or attractive for ever! Not only do attractive strategies get imitated by aggressive competitors but also—and perhaps more importantly—new strategic positions that undermine the attractiveness of our strategy keep emerging all the time.

Therefore, a company must never settle for what it has. While fighting it out in its current position, it must continuously search for new positions to colonize and new opportunities to take advantage of. The culture that any company must develop is that *strategies are not cast in concrete*. A company needs to remain flexible and ready to adjust its strategy if the feedback from the market is not favourable. More importantly, a company needs to continuously question the way it operates in its current position while still fighting it out in its current position against existing competitors. The key role that culture plays in strategy execution is a central theme of the book.

It is not easy to implement or change strategy. But books like this one—full of solid advice, new ideas, and real examples—can make the journey less onerous. Of course, knowing how to execute strategy is one thing, actually doing it is another! But at least the foundations for what action to take and how to do it are clearly spelled out in this wonderful book.

Introduction

A good plan violently executed now is better than a perfect plan executed next week.
—George Patton

Companies Spend Billions on Strategy

Every year companies spend billions of dollars on strategy guidance from some of the best brains on the planet. The consulting market in Europe alone is about $32 billion, and 12 percent of that goes on strategy consulting—a startling annual spend of $4 billion. The global annual spend, including everything from IT (information technology) to business strategy, reached about $415 billion in 2013, making the global spend on strategy consulting about $50 billion.[1] And that's only the start of the story. Think about how much money is spent on strategy conferences, on strategy retreats where executives meet to plan the future, on training courses in strategy, and on books on strategic planning. These might cause the figure to double.

McKinsey and other studies show that 70 percent of change initiatives fail—systems changes, culture changes, all the kinds of change that become inevitable when we want to embed a new strategy.[2] A *Harvard Business Review* collection of articles on change management published in 2011 suggested that as much as 90 percent of strategies fail to deliver their intended results, 95 percent of the workforce says they don't understand the company strategy and 70 percent fail at execution.[3]

So of that direct spend of $50 billion, we might as well put $35 billion in a pile and burn it.

Something fundamental is going wrong. We spend a fortune on strategy, but it doesn't work. Why not? The strategy provides the game plan, a way forward, a sense of direction and purpose. But we have overemphasized the role of strategy and under-estimated the critical role of execution. We need a strategy for execution.

On the Radar

Look on a ship's radar screen, and you will see an array of infor-mation. The radar signals reflect from the land and other large vessels to confirm your course and let you know about the obsta-cles to avoid. But the radar also detects weak signals that rebound from small boats and hidden dangers. It's not always easy to dis-tinguish these weak signals from the background noise, and it takes a skilled operator to recognize the small signs that indicate a potential risk.

It's the same in business. Leaders scan for weak signals that can signify danger or opportunity. If someone in North Dakota cancels an order, does it signify a larger problem? If an employee is tak-ing a lot of time off, does he have a personal issue or is it lack of engagement with the job? Is a drop in weekly sales an aberration or the beginning of a process of decline?

Having picked up a weak signal, the smart leader files it away, checks it out, triangulates information. Sometimes it is nothing. The signal disappears off the screen, and the corporate ship sails on untroubled.

But, once in a while, the signal grows in strength, it emerges through the cloudy mass of other signals, and it announces itself as something you need to pay attention to.

That's what happened with this book.

At the start of the decade we did some in-depth work with the top 80 executives of an international bank that employs more than 70,000 people. What struck us was how the executives referred to the bank in the third person—the bank does this, the bank insists on that. They were the top 0.1 percent. Who was the bank, if not them?

Strategy execution is surprisingly underresearched. People tend to focus on the creation of strategy and getting the strategy right rather than how it makes the leap to reality. Later, we came across some academic research surveying all the work on failure in strategy execution.[4] There was a glaring omission in the research. There was no mention of the role of the top level of executives in strategy execution.

What Happens When Leaders Don't Own It?

Over the last 30 years we have worked with leaders and organizations throughout the world. We have routinely been impressed by the intelligence and sheer energy of the people we encounter. They are driven, smart people who want to improve the performance of their organizations and of themselves.

But, despite this honest endeavour, there is often disappointment. Programs of change grind to a halt. Strategies are formulated, but then wither on the corporate vine. Bright ideas and initiatives disappear into the organizational ether.

What started out, just over 10 years ago, as a weak signal warning about the potential lack of felt ownership among the most senior leaders in one company has become a cacophony of sound. What was at first a light refrain has grown steadily into a chorus. The chorus is "Why don't they get it?" Or "They aren't moving fast enough." Sometimes it's "They lack ambition"; on other occasions, "They lack ownership."

The message is clear. For some reason, the executives at this critical level are not living up to the expectations held for them. And it's happening across a range of organizations and industries. In hundreds of conversations, thousands of executives have shared their stories of frustration with us and their colleagues.

The ownership and passion felt by the CEO isn't getting down to the next level. These are executives with considerable responsibility for running the business who wield tremendous power. They direct large units of the business. And they feel out of touch and out of control.

If the strategy cascade is getting stuck this high up, then the chance of implementing any strategy—however brilliant—is severely compromised. It just isn't going to happen. The true challenge to effective strategy execution today starts with the senior executives. Not the CEO and the executive team, but the leaders reporting to them.

Five Steps to Execution

Over the last five years we have focused our energies on trying to figure out why this happens and what the potential solutions are. We have interviewed executives worldwide and grilled many other attendees at our executive programs to get to the truth.

The result is *The Strategy of Execution*.

Like most executives, we realize that identifying a phenomenon is one thing. Doing something about it is the real challenge. *The Strategy of Execution* provides a five-step route forward for any leader stuck in the desolate corporate hinterland between great strategy and successful execution. CEOs are hired as strategists and fired for poor execution.

Step one starts with the critical but unexplored question of the surprising lack of ownership from top executives and ways to mend this. We call these senior executives the Village. We then move on to step two and consider how they can be better led by the CEO and executive team. We refer to this group as the Village Elders. The truth is that most strategies are overplanned and underled. At the heart of the book in step three we look closely at why executives continually and mistakenly try to lead an emotive topic like change with too much thinking. Rational analysis and objective feedback don't help someone who is scared of a different future to pick up their courage and move forwards. In step four we explain how to spread ownership of strategy execution through-out the whole organization, and in step five we focus on building endurance for the marathon of strategy execution. Then we offer a self-assessment guide in Chapter 6 so that that you can work out how ready your organization is to execute strategy well.

So the five steps are:

1. Mobilize the Village
2. Gather the Elders
3. Power-up feeling
4. Energize people
5. Build endurance.

Join us.

1

Mobilize the Village

Outstanding leaders go out of their way to boost the self-esteem of their personnel.
If people believe in themselves, it's amazing what they can accomplish.
—Sam Walton[1]

Cisco Gets It

Cisco was incorporated in December 1984 and headquartered in San Jose, California. Husband and wife Len Bosack and Sandy Lerner, both working for Stanford University, wanted to e-mail each other from their respective offices located in different buildings but couldn't. There was no technology that could deal with disparate local area protocols. They and other computer scientists designed a software system, the Internet Operating System (IOS), which could send streams of data from one computer to another. As a result of solving their challenge, the multiprotocol router was born. The software was loaded into a box containing microprocessors specially designed for routing and was then sold as a package to businesses.

Cisco is the plumber of the technology world, making routers, switches, IP telephony, data centers, mobile devices, and advanced network technologies that keep data moving "7/24" in Cisco vernacular. Customer demand led to an online customer support system by 1992 and by the mid-1990s, the company was providing consultancy services and customer-driven solutions.

In 2007, Cisco CEO John Chambers went to the World Economic Forum in Davos, Switzerland.[2] He was impressed with the quality of answers produced in a group exercise on a vision for life in 2015 and became convinced that top-down, command-and-control leadership and decision making had to stop. In April 2007 he repeated the exercise in Cisco and found that three different groups of employees came up with the same answer to a question about the company's mobile strategy. Chambers said, "You can take your top 40 or 50 people and then your top 300 and then your top 3,000 and still arrive at the same decisions."[3]

By 2009, Chambers had restructured Cisco into a series of 43 boards reporting to 12 councils, each with about 14 members, including 1 or 2 senior vice presidents or vice presidents. The 12 councils of 14 people (the top 168) reported into the operating committee, which was made up of the 15 top executives of the company, including Chambers. All board or council members had delegated authority for decision making from their function or business unit. What are the advantages to this approach? The leaders of business units formerly competing for power and resources now shared responsibility for one another's success. And their intimate role in reaching decisions meant that they felt that they owned execution of them.

Cowboys

In the company's old "cowboy culture," strong personalities were rewarded for jostling one another out of the way to get Chambers' approval. The internal economy of the old Cisco was very much market based. After the company was reorganized into boards and councils, executive compensation became based on how well the collective of businesses performed, not the executive's own individual product unit. Cisco vice president Ron Ricci said at the time, "One of the traditional ways you define power in a big corporation is by the resources you control. It's one of the evil characteristics of corporations. If you control resources for your unilateral use, you can move away from the greater whole, even if you make good decisions." CEO Chambers said, "I now compensate our leadership team based on how well they do on collaboration and the longer-term picture. If we take the focus off of how they did today, this week, this quarter, it will work."[4]

What John Chambers wanted was to create a company with less reliance on the CEO, less deference to hierarchy, and more widespread involvement in decision making. In addition to these features, what he also got was faster decisions, speedier resource allocation, and a more nimble company. His leaders, the top 168 sitting on councils, followed by the next 500 on boards, felt ownership of the decisions they had a hand in reaching and therefore acted on them faster. They adopted an enterprise-wide mindset, looking out for Cisco as a whole, not just their own part of the business.

We aren't seeing this in many organizations. Cisco is truly unusual. And it's what we are advocating here, as the first step in effective strategy execution.

It doesn't need to be done in the same way, of course. There is more than one organizational form that can garner ownership from the top 100 or so executives. But the objective is right.

Three Core Ideas

Moving from strategy to execution has always been tough. In other words, execution was never easy, and people who say otherwise are kidding you or themselves (and possibly both).

This book is not about how to get sign off on the strategy. That process involves the CEO, the executive team, the board, and a whole bunch of external stakeholders. It's important. Setting off without stakeholder buy-in is a risky business. Dominique Fournier offers us one example. He was CEO of Infineum, a research joint venture between Exxon and Shell, until 2012. Getting sign-off on the strategy takes a lot of hard work behind the scenes including lobbying in order to gain agreement so that you can move forward. You can't force decisions or implement ideas before they are fully accepted. Fournier did this once and found out the hard way that it was inadvisable. He moved to implement a strategic initiative that was right for Infineum, but he didn't have clear buy-in from the board. The initiative ended after 12 months, representing wasted effort, frustration, and loss of credibility in his leadership. "I think it was right for Infineum, but I was wrong to implement it without agreement. I had to undo everything—it was painful."[5]

This book is about how to execute strategy. Once you have sign-off on the strategy itself, how do you make it happen for real?

In this chapter, we focus on three core ideas. The first idea is that the root of the struggle to execute strategy has shifted over time. We used to think that incalcitrant workers at the bottom of the organization acted as a block. But today there is a growing awareness that the problem has shifted. Our work over many years in this field has convinced us that the strategy execution bottleneck has moved up several levels in the modern organization. It's not the CEO and it's usually not his or her immediate executive team either; they get it. Nor is it the people lower down the organization; they will execute the strategy if given proper leadership. The block to strategy execution today lies with the top 100 most senior executives. Why do we call it the *top 100*? It's an approximation. Sometimes more, or sometimes it's fewer, depending upon the size, nature, and geographic spread of the organization. For example, at CISCO it's about 160; at Rio Tinto, 120; at Whitbread, 40; and at Jaguar Land Rover, it's 160. Think in terms of the top 0.1–0.2 percent of the total population.

The second idea relates to this group of 100 top executives. We see them as a community, like a small village. And unless they embrace the strategy and actively engage with it, the strategy (any strategy) is doomed to failure. The third idea covers how to tackle the challenge and mobilize the top 100 to action.

So there you have it: three simple ideas. First, the biggest block on execution is the top 100 in the organization. Second, if they as a community don't actively support a strategy, it is dead in the water. Third, a few crisp ideas on how to undo the blockage and get these top 100 executives owning and moving the strategy to execution.[6] First, let's look at the evolution of the problem from the bottom to the top over the last 150 years.

The Shifting Problem

If we think about the first 70 or so years of the last century, any barrier to getting business done was firmly placed at the door of the workers. In fact, this bias stems from the industrial revolution. The most famous consultant of the late nineteenth and early twentieth centuries was Frederick Winslow Taylor,[7] who used engineering principles to increase productivity dramatically in factories. His underlying belief was that people were lazy and would take any opportunity they could to slack. He believed that they needed to be controlled by managers or experts (in the organizational principles he advocated) in order to get a good day's work out of them.

Middle Managers—Glue, Concrete, or Cooked Geese?

Who would volunteer to be a middle manager when these are the kind of labels used to describe you? By the 1980s, the blame had shifted up to middle managers, formerly considered to be the glue holding the organization together but now seen as the roadblock to success. This "layer of concrete" was blamed for failing to translate a perfectly good strategy from the top into actions and deliverables for the workers.[8] Roger Smith, chairman and CEO at General Motors from 1981, referred to middle managers as "the frozen middle."[9]

Leaders tried to eliminate middle managers by creating leaner, more empowered organizations with fewer layers that were focused on delivering service to customers. Tom Peters, who was the first management writer to have a management book reach the best-seller list and the first management expert to be called a guru, wrote, "Middle Management as we have known it since the railroads invented it after the Civil War is dead. Therefore middle managers as we have known them are cooked geese."[10]

The "cooked geese" ranks of middle managers were decimated during the 1980s and 1990s—and it's not over yet. *The Economist* had a recent article[11] featuring Unilever, the food and healthcare giant, in a story about consistently reducing layers of management from a startling 36 tiers at the start of this century to 6 levels today. As *The Economist* put it, "Rising through the grades at such places was often a reward for longevity, not competence. Many big firms simply accumulated managers over time. It is little surprise, therefore, that recent cost-cutting efforts have focused on the middle manager." But middle management and bureaucracy are not synonymous; it depends what they are expected to do. For example, we know that an individual's relationship with his or her line manager is critical to motivation and productivity.[12] A good manager can get extraordinary performance out of a team, while a bad manager makes people quit. Good people managers, with enough initiative to balance the needs of the company's day-to-day operations against the need to implement the wider strategy, can still play a valuable role in organizations today.

It may save money in the short run to cut middle managers, especially if you have let recruitment or promotion at this level get out of control, although many believe that the savings are illusory.[13] But there is no evidence that the organization gets any better at strategy execution with fewer middle managers. In fact, the opposite may happen. According to Wharton School faculty member Joe Ryan, "In cost-cutting times, knee-jerk reactions happen. There is a paradox where middle managers are essential, but end up sacked when restructuring occurs. It's a rough situation because the people needed to run the most important projects are in the middle."[14]

We believe that the problem with strategy execution today lies at the top—not with the workers or with middle managers. We call them the Village. Let's meet the inhabitants.

The Village

How do you become a member of the top 100 Village? You have to run a large part of the business. It may be a geographic area, a function, or a business unit. For example, you could be the global head of marketing, the general manager for India, or the CEO of gas compressors. You are a leader in your own right. You have responsibility for your financial results, and you lead strategy development in your part of the business. You may also contribute to the overall strategy for the organization. At a minimum you can expect to participate in the annual conference where the CEO presents and updates the strategy for the whole organization.

Why a Village?

If you look at how we human beings have historically structured our society, the basic building block is a village.[15] Anthropologists, such as Roger Dunbar, tell us that the optimum number of relationships we can deal with is about 150—the size of a small village.[16] This is now known as "Dunbar's number," and his work is fascinating. According to him, the current mean size of the human neocortex was developed about 250,000 years ago. It's the size of our brain that limits the number of meaningful relationships we can manage, or monitor, simultaneously. When a group's size exceeds this limit, it becomes unstable and begins to fragment. His surveys of village and tribe sizes back this up. The estimated population of a Neolithic farming village was 150; similarly, 150 represented the splitting point of Hutterite[17] settlements, and 150 was the basic unit size of professional armies in Rome and in modern times since the sixteenth century.

So if we want to create a close-knit community for action at the top of our organizations, 150 is about the maximum size that will work.

Some organizations choose structures that make good use of Dunbar's insight. Sir Richard Branson, founder of the Virgin Group of businesses, was famous for popularizing the idea in his early business empire in the 1970s, when he tried to keep business units to a size of about 150. He still believes in this today. Branson says, "The challenge as you get bigger is not to become so big that you become just like another one of the big carriers. Trying to stay small while getting bigger is very important. Any company that has more than 250 people in a building is in danger of starting to become impersonal. In an ideal world, 150 people are the most that should be working in one building and in one organization, so that everyone knows each other and knows their Christian names."[18]

The number of 150 also includes past relationships where you still want to keep in contact. Dunbar tells us that 150 would be the average group size only for communities with a very high incentive to remain together. For a group of 150 to remain cohesive, he speculates that as much as 42 percent of the group's time would have to be devoted to social grooming. And that's where the problem starts.

The Blockage in the Village

The difference between a real village and the top 100 Village in companies is that, in the real village, you live close to your neighbors and you know them—sometimes too well. You can look across the street and the village green and watch them as they go about their daily business. Your paths intertwine and cross, and conversations and pleasantries keep everyone in touch. Some stay and some depart, but newcomers are visible and are assimilated into the community.

In contrast, the top 100 Village is spread all over the organization and, in a global firm, all over the world. It's hard for the 100 executives to identify that they are part of a community with a special responsibility in strategy execution for the organization as a whole. They are separated, if not by geography, then by function or specialty, in their various roles as country heads or leaders of functions, services, or product lines. As one executive complained ruefully, "You tell us that we are the top 150, but we don't even see each other. We are not even a group. We hardly ever meet." He wanted to be part of a leading community for his organization, but he just couldn't see how it could be done. The Villagers may not even be the 100 most senior, as generally a few high-potential, but more junior executives, will be included. They mostly meet as a collective only once a year at a formal conference organized just for them. The objective of the conference is for the CEO to explain the strategy and present progress to date and to urge this group of executives on to greater effort. If the CEO and the executive team construct the strategy, this group makes it come alive. Without these people, nothing happens. But they don't see that.

Management in Retreat

Let's think about the norm in most organizations. The argument is that the top 100 Village knows who its members are only because they may meet once a year for a few days. This would be an annual two- to three-day gathering in a large hotel or conference center. Communicating information—about new ideas, products, strategies, opportunities, and challenges—would be a core objective. Generally, this takes the form of presentations from the stage. Between presentations there would be opportunities to mingle, either through formally designed sessions or informal events like lunch. All attendees wear a badge with their name on it, so everyone is able to address their colleagues by name, even though they may not know which part of the business the other is from or what she or he actually does. It's very unlikely that any one individual will manage to talk to all of the other 99 during this short period. They literally don't all meet each other during the event, let alone see themselves as a collective. There may be some social events, probably limited to dinner, or perhaps with the addition of a special event or outing. Whatever happens will definitely not meet Dunbar's definition of social grooming. Often, for security reasons the company will not list the members or their contact details, so unless you exchanged business cards during the meeting, you won't be able to get in touch again afterwards. They have a very long way to go in creating a real community for action.

So the core of the problem is that the members of this critical group of executives don't see themselves as a community at all. Spread out as they are across the business, with considerable personal accountabilities, they are intent on delivering results in their part of the world. And just in their part of the world. For the business to achieve its strategic goals, they have big stretch targets accompanied by the ambition to succeed. They are driven to deliver the results expected of them.

Yet they have no sense of collective responsibility and accountability. They don't see or understand the power they can wield as a group. They do not understand the opportunity they have to act as a force for good. They see themselves as individuals, in turn directing and defending their part of the business, with their teams, under instruction or exhortation from the top. The strategy briefing to them is a means of tuning in to their personal boundaries for action, not an opportunity to challenge, reshape, and own the deliverables identified for the organization as a whole. They do not see themselves as enterprise-wide leaders.

It's a Conundrum

The CEO looks down and sees the community that must be mobilized to deliver the strategy. That's why the company goes to the expense of flying in the executives for the strategy retreat. The community, however, doesn't see itself at all; not even as a virtual village.

So we have a conundrum. The Village members don't see themselves as a community for collective action, but the CEO and executive team see them as pivotal to execution. And execution, to be successful, has to be coordinated among these significant players. It's not the CEO's job to play referee, so coordination implies collaboration across the Village. But a member of the Village, by definition, holds down a big job and has more than enough to do every day, without worrying about being part of a virtual community, collaborating with people he or she meets only once a year, if that. How can we help the members of the Village to care? How can it become a core part of the Villager's job?

Align in the Sand

To execute a strategy efficiently and effectively, there has to be agreement around common goals, at every level of the business. First there is consensus at the top, which needs to become alignment among the members of the top 100 Village. The alignment must then turn into collaboration further down the organization. Yet as long as I see myself as a lone leader, for example, running the business operations in India, then I will see it as my role to do the best for India, not for the whole enterprise. So I may make decisions and act in ways that are good for India, but maybe not for the rest of the business. If I could see myself as part of a powerful community of the top 100 leaders who must act in unison if the strategy is to succeed, then I might be more inclined to act in ways that move the whole organization forward, not just my part of it. I already have the freedom to play my own way in my own sandpit, but in order to storm the beach, we must come together as a unified community.

It's a real challenge to get 100 people (or 70, or 150, depending on the size of your Village) aligned. But it can be done.

Getting the Village to Work

Irene Dorner has been president and CEO of HSBC America since October 2011. In 2013, HSBC was the world's third-largest publicly held bank and the sixth-largest public company.[19] HSBC is a big, complex business in an industry still mired in the aftermath of the 2008 financial crisis. Leading HSBC America has its own set of unique problems started by the purchase of Household in

November 2002. At the time, this was widely acclaimed as a smart strategic move. In a 2003 cover story, *The Banker* noted, "When banking historians look back, they may conclude that [it] was the deal of the first decade of the 21st century."[20] By 2009, then HSBC chairman Stephen Green was publicly stating that, in retrospect, HSBC should not have acquired Household International.[21]

Dorner shares the issues she and her own Village (in her case, the top 120) faced in their challenges to change the culture and to execute the strategy:

> *I inherited a challenging situation when I arrived, with undeclared business problems and a poor culture underpinned by various other bad practices. There were three companies (two subsidiaries and a holding company), each had a CEO, one of whom was me. Authority and responsibility were too dispersed. I only took control of all of the businesses in October 2011 and then felt real ownership. In February 2012 I held a leadership conference for the top 120 executives. At that time, none of the business units could articulate each other's strategies and nor could the support functions. I allowed an amnesty period and forgave everyone for not knowing the strategy—we had no elevator version of it. Normally, not knowing the strategy is a serious flaw.*[22]

Get a Credible Story Out There

Dorner's first act was to gather the Village. She understood the problem, that not all of these leaders understood the strategy as a whole, nor their contribution to it. Like a level 5 leader, she took the blame for it, because she felt that she had not communicated it clearly.[23] She started getting the message out, to get alignment in the Village. Her messaging was positive, looking at the business challenges as a burning platform for change and the basis for future success, rather than as the end of the line. She's very clear about the value of the Village. Dorner further says, "You cannot execute your strategy unless you are seen as credible and can paint the picture and tell the story to this most senior group." The first step in getting alignment didn't go altogether smoothly. Villagers were given a copy of the PowerPoint presentations from the meeting, in the expectation that they would go away and present them to their distributed teams. Only a few did so.

What Gets Measured Gets Done

Undaunted, Dorner convened a second conference in September 2012, seven months later, where she explained the strategy again and launched a culture change program. This time, when the PowerPoint presentations were handed out, she made her expectations clearer—using them to brief teams back at work was mandatory. She even scripted the strategic messages for the top 120, ready-made to be communicated to the next level. And, as in all thorough execution processes, she checked whether it had been done by surveying the employees to whom the message should have been passed. So there was pressure on the top 120 to make this communication happen. Downward pressure from her as the CEO; upward pressure from the people reporting directly to them, who didn't want to hear from colleagues that they were missing messages being passed to others; and pressure from peers in the top 120 because any lack of action was visible and measurable.

Dorner's story is typical in its recognition of the pivotal role played by the top 100. While she inherited business challenges on many fronts, she was quick to acknowledge that getting buy-in from the Village was central to executing the strategy and changing the culture. The business units and the functions understood their part of the jigsaw puzzle but couldn't see the overall picture of the business as a whole and so couldn't understand the broader context within which they were making decisions. They didn't understand each other's roles, and they struggled to articulate the strategy. So nothing was moving. As time passed, people had lost confidence in their ability to deliver, so she had to be careful to tell the story of the strategy as a way of proving what could be achieved, and not as a means of frightening people about what was stuck. She described a burning platform for improvement, not a crisis.

She also offered a period of amnesty, again so that people gained confidence and were not blamed for their inability to articulate a strategy that she herself felt had been poorly communicated. Dorner believes that not knowing the strategy at this senior level is a serious executive flaw. She continues to convene the members of the Village twice a year, with plenty of contact, including polling their direct reports, in between meetings. How's it going? Headquarters has noticed and is starting to ask how she achieved the alignment and buy-in she has garnered. Nothing breeds confidence like success. Dorner says, "Ninety percent are now on board. We are serious, we can do it, and we have proved it."

Another Industry, Another Village

David Levin is the CEO of UBM, a multinational media company headquartered in London. The history of the companies that now make up UBM stretches back almost 200 years to the founding of the *Journal of Commerce*, first published by Samuel Morse in 1827. Today, the *Journal of Commerce* is still produced in both print and digital formats by UBM Global Trade. UBM businesses still publish many other titles that were launched in the nineteenth century, including *Building* magazine, launched in 1843 by Joseph Hansom. The company was founded in 1918 as United Newspapers by David Lloyd George in order to acquire the *Daily Chronicle* and *Lloyd's Weekly Newspaper*. It took the name United Business Media in 2000, when it sold the *Daily Express* to Richard Desmond. Levin talks about what strategy execution means to him:

> *In leading this culture change, all my attention has been focused on the front line leaders, the ones who have to go over the top and persuade others to follow. This means focusing on the top 70–100 people in the business and getting them to really buy in,*

with a holistic approach. We discuss the strategy and we focus on alignment and values and then ensure they have the authority and autonomy to make things happen. So I initially focus on this 1.5 percent of the total population of 6,500. It has worked. If you look at our internal staff surveys, the commitment and ownership of this level is significantly statistically much higher than everyone else in UBM and higher than the global benchmark average. Indeed, we even see that echoed with higher scores among their direct reports.[24]

Here again we feel the power and impact of the CEO focusing on the most senior and influential executives to turn the first lever of strategy execution. Get their support, and it has a ratchet effect on the rest of the organization. Levin sees it as a vital part of his job to sell change to his top 70 Village so that the Villagers feel excited and inspired. Then they can explain it to the levels below them, who have to execute with the same sense of engagement. He even makes it his business to measure their levels of commitment so that he can test if he is getting it right. Like Dorner, he follows through. As he requests their ownership for the strategy, he makes it clear to them that he is looking after UBM only for a period and expects to pass the leadership baton to them. He encourages their direct input to the UBM strategy in order to increase their feeling of ownership and to urge them to be proactive.

Incredible Leadership

Both CEOs, Levin and Dorner, understand the pivotal role of the Village as the first and most critical step in strategy execution. The top 100 have to move with you. Not everyone is as thorough as they are in precise action and follow through. There is often an implicit expectation that executives as senior as these need only a course of action mentioned and they will immediately get onto it. This is not the case. It's not because they are slow-witted or have malicious intentions. If that were the case, it's highly unlikely that they'd reach or remain in the Village. It's more that life is busy, they have big business agendas of their own, and they'll "get around to it one day." And it's because far too many of their leaders underestimate the importance of the personal touch and the power of communicating directly and often with people about what they need to do to make strategy happen.

Sometimes the CEO and executive team may even hinder rather than help. One CEO took very poor advice about his role at the annual strategy conference. A dry, thoughtful, and intellectual man, he was encouraged to jump off the stage at the end of his presentation, strike a guitar pose, and shout, "Let's rock!" The move was greeted with stunned silence. In another company, the executive team had developed an exciting new strategy. The company was really well placed to globalize; it had leading edge technology backed by new products and an enviable reputation. The story was going to be a great one, and people were excited to hear it. Amazingly, there had been no leaks about the strategy, which was to be launched at an extravagant offsite location in Greece. The top 300 leaders were assembled in a theater and, in complete darkness, the uplifting music started. The faces of the executive team were haloed in light and then returned to darkness, as they each took their dramatic turn to speak from their places on the stage to tell the story of the new strategy. The atmosphere, which started out as electric, slowly turned to farce. The CEO took the first turn and was riveting, his face lit from underneath, as he presented with passion, conviction, and verve. The CFO who followed him clearly felt awkward with the presentation style, but did his best—he was a bit like an uncoordinated dad dancing at a wedding. Next it was the turn of the sales director, who was clearly competing with the CEO to be the most effective performer of the night. As head after head was lit from below the chin and then returned to darkness, the story was lost in translation. Going global was a big step and needed careful selling, but its credibility was lost in the theatricality of the event. Polite applause in the room was followed by disbelieving and unnerved conversation in small groups later. No sale.

We shouldn't expect the Village to simply follow. It takes work and concentration. The Villagers hold the key to success or failure of strategy execution. Helping them to understand their important role shows them the way forward. It's the difference between their acting as permafrost or as the thin active layer on top of permafrost.[25] If they are frozen, nothing else is going to move.

When Permafrost Rules

When it's badly done, it's ugly. Let's go back to the example of running a region as one of the top 100. If I am CEO India, it will obviously be important to me to understand the broader corporate strategy. I may embrace or resist it, but I will certainly pay attention to key messages from the worldwide CEO and headquarters. But if I make a decision that benefits India but creates a disadvantage for South Africa or Indonesia, I will be less perturbed. It will be less visible to me. I will probably know the CEO of the South African business, but not that well, so I will probably lack the compunction or guilt that might accompany letting down a friend. And I will more than likely expect headquarters to mediate or make a different decision if people there want to try to countermand mine (but I am a pretty powerful player and can get away with a lot in my region).

Let's fast-forward to the annual strategy conference, where I may never meet the CEO of the South African business at all (100 is a pretty crowded room, and we have only two days together). Let's remain optimistic and say that we do get a chance to meet. We may not have much opportunity to discuss whatever happened when our strategies collided because we are busy hearing about the new strategy and moving from CEO speech, to CFO briefing, to breakout sessions in different combinations of groups of our peers. If we do discuss what happened, it is likely to be a short discussion and probably quite a defensive one. So our clash is either not dealt with at all or dealt with hastily and superficially. And it's not just the big strategic issues that get in the way. It's not unusual for regions or business units within the same company to compete with each other for the same customer, even cutting prices against each other to try and secure the sale. Customers complain about several sales representatives from the same company visiting them sequentially, offering different packages at different prices. One executive said, "Sometimes it feels a lot easier to work with outside partners than it does with colleagues inside the business."

It's been a long time since Lew Platt, the former chief executive (1992–1999) of Hewlett-Packard, said, "If only HP knew what HP knows, we would be three times more productive,"[26] but it looks like the same inability to share and collaborate is alive and well in business today. Can we improve on this? How can we help the Village members act as one community?

So far, we have covered the first two stages in Mobilizing the Village—locating and identifying the top 100 Village and offering some examples of CEOs who have moved their Villagers to act in concert. Let's move on to the third and final idea in this chapter: some generalizable heuristics for getting the Village owning and moving the strategy to execution.

Getting the Village Moving

There are several aspects to getting the Village moving. We need to make the villagers visible to each other as a community and check that the Village has the right inhabitants. We then need to help them feel ownership for strategy execution through giving them a voice in shaping the strategy itself. Some Villagers will need to be sold one by one and others may need to be appropriately challenged if they undermine execution. Sometimes their execution efforts will need to be protected from attack by others. And finally, we need to ensure that they have both the will and the capability to execute. Let's look first at making the Village visible.

Make Them Visible
The first aspect in mobilizing the Village is to help the members of this important community see each other.

One annual retreat for a couple of days is inadequate, especially when too often the communication is one way. It's a download from the top on what needs to be done in the coming year. So meet more than once a year, for a little longer than two days. Restructure the sessions so that the Village members have time to talk to each other about what really matters. The argument against this is always, "We can't afford to be out of the office for so long." How can you afford not to be out of the office, when gaining understanding and alignment is the only way to move the company forward without everyone tripping over each other? Change the way you think about the role of this key group and the conferences they attend. See it as core and essential work, not something to fit in that gets in the way of "real" work.

Identify this group as a community and as a powerful force for good, and then assign them the responsibility of delivering the strategy for the organization as a whole. It's not just about the physical meetings of the Village, although these help to cement personal relationships. It's about being identified as a community, with special rights and responsibilities. The members might be on the CEO's speed dial or have their own section on the company intranet. They might be the CEO's sounding board. Messages to them should be about their unique position and collective role in enabling strategy execution, in a way that cannot be achieved at the levels above or below them. Tom Albanese, until early 2013 the CEO of the mining giant, Rio Tinto, would hold regular conference calls with subgroups of leaders at this level. He was checking in, feeling the pulse of the business, talking about what was important on his mind, and getting the same in return.

Get the Right People in the Circle

Tom Albanese led Rio Tinto as CEO for almost six years, from May 2007 until early 2013. Rio Tinto was founded in 1873 and at the time he left was one of the top three mining companies in the world by value.[27] Albanese steered Rio Tinto safely through the purchase of Alcan, a hostile takeover bid from BHP Billiton, and a challenging attempt to diversify business and shareholdings to China—the third move heavily disputed by Australian shareholders. He is a thoughtful strategist, a hater of conflict, and a huge believer in working hard on getting buy-in from senior executives. An original thinker, Albanese offers a different perspective on the Village:

> Corporations have become more efficient by creating global functions, such as Compliance, Health & Safety, and Procurement—more efficient, because these functions safeguard deep expertise and apply global systems that save duplication and thus resources. But at the same time globalization has created a more difficult structure for strategy development and propagation. Because of the global functions, a higher percentage of top managers now see the world through a fairly narrow functional lens. At the same time, fewer line managers can take an holistic view of the business (they have to take or follow advice from the core functions), so they become less helpful in creating the strategy.[28]

This is an interesting perspective. In a global organization, it makes sense to create global systems and functions. Why? Let's take human resources (HR) as an example, the function that looks after employees. If you want your workforce to be mobile so that you can move people to where in the world the work needs them, then it makes sense to have one global set of employment rules. Without this, you get duplication, as each country invents its own rules and ways of working. You get discrepancies: for example, if I move to another country, the new employing country may pay me different allowances from those I got in the last country, or even offer me a different level of pay—which means I may not wish to move, if the pay is lower, or push to move unnecessarily, if the pay I will be offered is higher.

In the worst case, in some companies employees have to resign from one legal entity to join another within the same company. This wastes time and resources and diminishes an employee's motivation to move, because whatever the promises, resigning feels risky. So the arguments for creating global functions are compelling. One global HR policy, administered by one function, can iron out such discrepancies. But what do you lose in the process? First, there are more functional heads among the key top 100 executives, whose job is to support, rather than implement, the strategy. And you lose the contribution to, and ownership of, the strategy from the people who actually run the business. Their hands are tied because they have to comply with global rules and they lose control and oversight of the whole business. Taken to the extreme, the functions could become so powerful that they put the brakes on strategy execution, as the whole business has to dance too slowly to global rules that may not suit every region (do the same rules work in the United States and China?). Albanese makes the valid point that the top 100 may not be the right 100.

Less Is More

Albanese continues:

> *The top 100 was a top 50 ten years ago, because more functions have been taken out of the hands of the line managers who actually run the business and put in the hands of the functional heads. (Of the Rio top 120, about 50 percent are functional heads.) Worse, the line managers have to consult, and spend time selling into, the functions. This is a huge overt and covert overhead. The top group are more effective as a cost structure, but less effective as the centre for strategy and execution in the organization.*[29]

So it's about balancing the upside and downside of global functions. The upside is cost saving. (Actually, this also deteriorates over time, as each region needs at least one functional employee to deal with the global function in headquarters and, like Topsy in *Uncle Tom's Cabin*,[30] the number employed for this purpose in the region tends naturally to grow over time.) The downside is loss of strategic ownership and slowed execution. What if we got the top

100 down to 50 or 60? It would probably still need to include some functions, like human resources, because the head of this function is central to building the people capability that the organization needs. Taking Rio as an example, with about 75,000 employees, a top 60, rather than a top 120, would reduce the Village from 0.1 percent to 0.08 percent of the total population, hardly a dramatic loss of representation. The smaller number would be much easier to work with. There would be more opportunities for discussion and debate, it would be easier to incorporate their ideas into the strategy, and it would be simpler to get them together more often.

We started with the heart of Albanese's message—choose carefully whom you pick as your top 100. The idea has now expanded. The question of whether the top 100 includes the right people has now become a question of whether the top 100 is too big a number. Maybe the primary group should be made up of business leaders and high-potential leaders able to focus on a few strategically important issues? We need them to own the strategy because they will then be more committed to its execution.

Back Chat

All Villagers need to see that part of their role is to play nicely with their colleagues. If some fail to contribute and own the strategy that others have signed up for, the execution of the strategy will be seen as an option, not a conviction. We will start to see factions and alliances between those who believe in the journey and those who do not. As the nonparticipators seek to justify their alienation, they will send different messages and act in discord with their colleagues. The strategy will start to mutate, and strategic imperatives will lose clarity and become fuzzy. In the short term, the company will lose because the results that could have been achieved if everyone had pulled together will not be realized. In the longer term, the damage is more subversive. The tentative sense of community, so hard to sustain across geographic, functional, and time-zone boundaries, will start to dissipate. Those who have

participated wholeheartedly will become disillusioned and disheartened. You can guarantee that next year, it will be even harder
to get alignment behind execution of the strategy. What we need is
ownership across the whole Village, from each and every Villager.

What's the best way to get ownership? It's to let the Villagers
have a voice in shaping the strategy. Voice brings a sense of ownership.[31] Of course, you can allow time to solicit their reactions to
strategy presentations made at the annual conference, but it's more
serious than that. It needs a consistent process. One IT company
with 250,000 employees runs an internal equivalent of Facebook,
with 60,000 people online at any one time. Anyone can put in a
request for ideas and get responses. If it can be done with 250,000,
a space set aside on the company intranet for 150 people should
be easily replicable.

Karina Robinson is CEO of Robinson Hambro, which is a U.K.-
based executive search firm that specializes in recruiting board
members and in supporting chairmen. In this work, she meets a
lot of CEOs. Here's her advice. "The CEO and three close advisors actually create the strategy, but then the smart ones socialize
it with the top 100. Not all together, but in conversations with
small groups. The CEO talks it through so they feel ownership."[32]
It sounds like a recipe for mayhem, with 100+ voices involved
in strategy creation—the proverbial animal created by committee,
which ends up being a camel. Robinson is sanguine: "The CEO
has an inbuilt advantage and will be listened to. So they will only
change things at the margin."[33] What sounds like a risky gambit
becomes a sensible way of ensuring that the people pivotal to
moving strategy to execution understand and validate the overall
direction. They also have the opportunity to act as a reality check,
because sometimes, ideas that look great on paper can turn out to
be almost impossible to implement. Their voices have been heard
and now they own the ideas and will execute without needing to
be supervised or driven.

Nick Forster is COO of Reed Exhibitions, a division of Reed
Elsevier plc, which is an FTSE 100 company based in over

200 locations. Reed Exhibitions has a growing portfolio of 500 events in 39 countries, including trade and consumer exhibitions, conferences, and meetings, ranging across 44 industry sectors, from aerospace and aviation to beauty and cosmetics to sports and recreation. Forster agrees: "How strategy is created is certainly a large part of the problem. Strategy is the short term enactment of the CEO's vision, put together with a small team. It needs to include a bigger group and you need to pull out the key people to be involved."[34]

Selling Them One at a Time

Forster also sees one-to-one persuasion as a means of getting buy-in. "The top 100 do need to see the bigger picture and think further out into the future and longer term than they generally do. But you need to identify where the actual roadblocks are. Early involvement is critical to ownership. You never get 100 percent believers, but you need to pick people off—start with the believers. How do you spot who to target? You need to know your people—get out and visit them, have informal conversations with them and use your gut instinct."[35]

Forster is drawing a distinction between blanket communications with the top 100 in a conference setting and targeting specific individuals within the group for special treatment. He also suggests looking for the executives who buy in early and working with them to leverage their conviction. The CEO can't do it alone; you need advocates in the system.[36] The early believers who will spread the word and persuade others on your behalf, without instruction, they simply believe in what you are doing. To spot the advocates requires a honed instinct for people, insight into their beliefs, and a strong enough relationship to have the conversation you need with them without awkwardness. Forster has this finely honed instinct and loves spending time with people. To be honest, not every senior leader is equally sensitive, and you'll need a game plan if you lack good instincts with people.

Crystal Clear

Part of the communication issue is about the clarity and conviction of the CEO's message. As Irene Dorner advised earlier, the CEO needs to be credible and articulate in messages to the Village. But the messages can't stop at the Village borders, or the rest of the organization won't follow. Overall accountability for the strategy is held by the CEO and the executive team working alongside him or her, not with the Village members. How do you signal clearly to everyone that the CEO, executive team, and Village are all aligned? Back again to Dorner, who suggests, "Think about execution very visually at this level. They must face you to receive the message and then physically turn round to face the wider organization. Then they must touch base again, update, by turning back to face me."[37] She is recommending a constant flow of debate and communication, to and fro, visible to the wider organization, to simultaneously achieve and signal alignment.

The late Colin Marshall, who was CEO of British Airways from 1983–2004, played a central role in turning the company around from a widely disparaged, publicly owned entity to one of the world's most popular airlines in the 1980s.[38] He was well-known for using visual imagery in his turnaround of British Airways. At one of his top 100 conferences, after the presentations were finished, he and the others on the stage turned their backs to the audience, creating the image of an airplane, with Marshall in the pilot's seat, with everyone aligned behind him. As Dorner says, it must be visual: get them to face you, and then physically turn around and pass on the exact same message to those behind them.

Challenge Them When You Need To

It's not always going to be straightforward, and not everyone will be easy to persuade.

One CEO tells the story of a year-long journey to create a new strategy, involving consultants, away-days, and workshops. He had done everything he possibly could to ensure wall-to-wall buy-in from the top 60. He's good with people and watches them closely, so he had spotted the uncertain, the waverers, and the discontented. He worked with them to bring them on board. The transition was going to be painful for some, as the organization was restructured from functional silos into customer-facing business units. The balance of power was upset, and new hires were mixed in with lifelong employees to help to break deadlocks in parts of the business. Toward the end of the preparation period, just before launch, the CEO realized that he hadn't convinced a key player. This man wasn't the most senior in the top 60 group, but he was influential—people listened to him.

The CEO said: "I looked around the room. I could sense and smell the degree of conviction as I scanned from face to face. And then, I looked at his face. And I could see he hadn't got it. The subtle behavioral clues that revealed he had been acting his support. Why hadn't he come back to me? Why hadn't he reached out to his colleagues? I had created endless opportunities for all of them individually and collectively to challenge the plan, the assumptions, the logistics, the key players, and the consequences. Why had he not declared? More importantly, why had I not seen it?"

We think that this CEO is being pretty tough on himself. There are a lot of people to convince; it's easy to overlook one. Sadly, he had overlooked the wrong one. The good news is that he spotted it in time. But now, what to do next? Leave it and hope that the executive is swept along in the tide of change, that the momentum will be enough to carry him along after all? Tempting thought. And at the same time, a dangerous thought. The CEO was essentially about to go live on the biggest strategic change the company had ever faced, and a key player, an influential player, was not convinced. Let's get back to the story of a former CEO:

This was such a tough call. What to do? Should I proceed when I had a loose cannon in the core team, or confront him, with the possibility of a messy and probably public explosion just at the point of launch? His part of the organization was business critical

*to our long term competitive advantage. I chose confrontation—
privately, calling him in for a one-to-one chat. We talked about a
whole range of topics and I made it an easy conversation for him
while moving the discussion onto how we could secure the best
contribution from him in the most commercially productive way.
He owned up. He said he wanted to be left alone to do the work he
loved and not be swept up in all the noise of change.*[39]

The confrontation ended well in this story. The executive was
let go and then rehired as a consultant, so he could do the work
he enjoyed, but without having to buy in to the bigger strategic redirection, which he disliked. What if it hadn't gone well?
Should our CEO still have pursued the showdown? Emphatically
yes. There might have been a public battle, an open dispute, or
an attempt at mutiny, with the executive recruiting others to his
cause. But it would have been done, closed as a challenge—the
CEO has ultimate power. The other route, with a disbeliever running around the organization, would have meant a longer, more
covert, battle with a less certain outcome. The damage caused
would have been widespread and harder to contain. We are back
to the Dunbar challenge. How do we build and preserve a sense
of community so that the Village members have a strong incentive
to play nicely together?

Run Air Cover[40]

The CEO and executive team need to get stuff out of the way—
that is, remove obstacles that could slow or halt the Villagers. One
big obstacle is always the measuring stick used to reward individuals. If the system is set so that targets are individual or business-
unit based, the incentive will be to maximize your own and to
worry less if this has a bad effect on someone else's results. The
aim here is to encourage enterprise-wide leadership, so that people care more about the whole than the individual parts. Smooth
execution results from everyone working well together, across the
whole enterprise. How do we achieve this?

Collaboration Targets

There are a couple of ways to get people to care about organizational targets as well as their own. One is to define what collaboration looks like in your situation, both behaviors and practices, and measure the Villagers on these. Measures can be hard or soft, but once the data are gathered, act on them clearly. Too frequently, senior executives exhort behavior that is not rewarded in practice. For example, if you say collaboration is important, but then reward people for achieving outstanding business revenues despite the fact that it's clear they haven't collaborated, this signals that collaboration isn't so important after all. It's really about striking a balance between rewarding *what* is achieved as well as *how* it was done. It's also about thinking long and short term. Short-term results can be achieved with bad behavior and without due consideration of colleagues, but this will damage commitment and morale in the long term.

Another option to combine successfully individual with enterprise-wide effort is double counting. This is controversial and some organizations hate it, while others have operated with it successfully for years. Essentially, a business result is attributed in some measure to the units that collaborated to make it happen. You can see that, depending on how cleverly this is done, the worst-case scenario could be that the company pays out twice for the same activity, which it won't be able to afford over the long term. So it has to be done thoughtfully. One clever way we have seen this done is where one party gets the financial reward, while the collaborating partner gets the recognition.

The underlying principle is that you can't ask for a one-enterprise outlook and reward individual endeavor, and then still hope that you get collaboration.[41] You won't.

Training Wheels

Of course, it's not enough for the Villagers to be able to see each other and to believe in the same vision and direction. They will volunteer only if they believe that they are capable of contributing and making a difference, so ongoing development for these executives is important. Encourage training. It's too easy to believe that once you are a Villager there is nothing left to learn (or at least to guard your ego by pretending that there is nothing more that you can learn). It's not just about updating your technical or interpersonal skills; it's also about building self-confidence.

Summary

In this opening chapter, we describe the most senior level of the hierarchy, the top 100, as the level that is the most critical to strategy execution. We explain how, as management theory has evolved, it has become clear that the block to strategy execution is not with the general workforce, or with much-reviled middle managers, but sits instead with the top 100 executives in the organization. Getting their buy-in is critical in moving from strategy to execution, in bringing the strategy alive, and in making it happen.

We also look at how to mobilize the top 100, by making them visible as a Village, or community, to themselves and to the rest of the organization; how to get the right people in the Village; how to help them to feel real ownership for the strategy and its execution; and then how to remove obstacles from their path.

Throughout this chapter, we talk about the Village as though its members report directly to the CEO, but they don't. They are close enough to the CEO to know and interact with him or her—the messages tend to be passed directly. But there is another important group within the Village. This is the executive team that sits closest to the CEO, as advisors, advocates, and supporters. These people are generally known as the executive committee, because they make decisions about the strategy and lead execution for the organization. We see them as the Village Elders. We turn to their role in the next chapter. How do we ensure that the critical top 100 in the Village community are well led by the Village Elders?

2

Gather the Elders

A genuine leader is not a searcher for consensus, but a molder of consensus.
—Martin Luther King

Whatever Happened at Nokia?

Nokia was until recently a legend of adaptability and survival. The predecessors of the modern Nokia were the Nokia Company (Nokia Aktiebolag), Finnish Rubber Works Ltd (Suomen Gummitehdas Oy), and Finnish Cable Works Ltd (Suomen Kaapelitehdas Oy). Nokia started in 1865 when mining engineer Fredrik Idestam established a groundwood pulp mill on the banks of the Tammerkoski rapids in the town of Tampere in southwestern Finland in the Russian Empire and started manufacturing paper. They've come a long way. In that journey, Nokia followed some obvious moves, such as entering the telecom industry in the 1970s, like many other electrical equipment firms (it made insulated cables). It also survived crisis along the way. The company was in significant trouble in the late 1980s. Nokia had supplied high-tech electronic goods to the Soviet bloc in exchange for the raw materials it used to make tires and plastics. The fall of the Soviet bloc in 1989, and that of the Soviet Union two years later, meant that Soviet demand plummeted, halving the size of Nokia's telecom business and shattering its plans for international expansion.[1] However, Nokia recovered, and by 2006 it was the market leader with a share of 49.4 percent. It was the number-one global brand for mobile handsets and was so fashionable that, when sur-veyed, teenagers thought Nokia was a Japanese company. Nokia was the handset to have. But did Nokia's very recovery lay the groundwork for failing again? Years of repeated growth and suc-cess dangerously built into an orthodoxy—a fixed mindset that began shaping the decisions and judgment calls of the leadership team. Ben Wood, analyst at CCS Insight: "Complacency had kicked in. They felt they could do no wrong."[2] Then in January 2007, the market changed forever when Apple launched their iPhone. Nokia tried to respond but its Symbian operating system was inferior. Sales fell away dramatically. By 2011 Nokia had partnered with Microsoft to build the Windows Phone as a brand but still could not recover, and by 2013 its market share had shrunk to 3 percent.

After 148 years of successful trading and major transitions over the decades, Nokia was struggling. Its share price fell from a high of US $40 in late 2007 to under US $2 in mid-2012, and on June 18, 2012, Moody's downgraded Nokia's rating to junk (Zack.com). That same month, Nokia CEO[3] Stephen Elop admitted that the company's inability to foresee rapid changes in the mobile phone industry was one of the major reasons for the problems the com-pany was facing. On September 3, 2013 Microsoft agreed to buy Nokia's mobile phone business for $7.2 billion, with the deal to be finalized in early 2014, subject to approval by Nokia shareholders. The BBC leader read, "From market domination to sell-off in less than 10 years."[4] The sale of Nokia to Microsoft was a huge blow to Finnish national pride. Nokia chairman Risto Siilasmaa drew on the company's long history of transformation as a cause for opti-mism when he said, "Today marks a day of reinvention for Nokia. This is the beginning of the next 150 years of the Nokia story."[5]

Was It a Technology Miss?

One part of the explanation is definitely about technology, and much of it is on public record thanks to transparent statements from CEO Elop and copious press and business school cover-age. When the iPhone hit the market in January 2007, Nokia had prototype equivalents in varying stages of development but chose to launch the N95 handset. From one standpoint, it was probably the right decision, as it was technically superior to the iPhone. The N95 was a huge success, which brought an income stream that only helped to mask underlying problems with other products. But from a technology standpoint, it was a misstep. One of Nokia's recently departed executives told us, "We thought we were a phone company and actually we were a computer company. It's not about the handset, it's about eco-systems. Samsung has Android, and Apple has Apple, and those two together make the most profit of all mobile phones. Microsoft systems on phones is brilliant, but no one's using it so no one's developing it."

In September 2010, Stephen Elop joined Nokia from Microsoft, replacing Olli-Pekka Kallasvuo as CEO and becoming the first non-Finnish director in Nokia's history. In February 2011, a scathing internal memo from Elop was leaked, in full, to the press.[6] In it, he covered some of the technical challenges facing Nokia. "The first iPhone shipped in 2007, and we still don't have a product that is close to their experience. Android came on the scene just over 2 years ago, and this week they took our leadership position in smartphone volumes. Unbelievable."

It's a Leadership Issue

But Elop also alluded to internal leadership challenges in Nokia. "How did we get to this point? Why did we fall behind when the world around us evolved? I believe at least some of it has been due to our attitude inside Nokia. I believe we have lacked accountability and leadership to align and direct the company through these disruptive times. We're not collaborating internally."

One of the former top 100 Villagers expands on this:

The leadership team lacked credibility. The memo from Elop set out the burning platform for change, but the new strategy wasn't released until two days later. So we had no vision to tell us which way to jump from the platform, just a scathing catalog of errors. When the new strategy was unveiled to a conference of the top 200, it came as no surprise to us that our Symbian operating system was at last going to be replaced. I did a project for the Executive Committee in 2005, highlighting how we were even then struggling with the system. They acknowledged then that they were making some changes, but they weren't big enough or fast enough. No, our surprise and concern was that the leadership team who had got us into this mess was to remain largely unchanged. Complacency was a real problem. There was open dispute among the top 100 over the direction we were taking as a company. They never got our belief or buy-in.[7]

This is one person's opinion, not a scientific study or piece of research. But if even one of the Villagers reports this depth of disenchantment with the leadership team, strategy execution is going to be in trouble. The messages from the Elders have to be heartfelt to get the Village believing. They have to be credible to get the Village moving.

We end the last chapter by saying that the Village must be well led. In this chapter we investigate what that means. If we want the strategy to work in practice, we need the members of the very top team, the team sitting above the key 100, to see it as their primary job to persuade and enable the Village to move to action. Not to execute themselves, but to focus on governance, strategy creation, and moving others to action. The challenge we face is that the way most leaders are developed means that by the time they reach the most senior positions, they are uniquely ill-qualified for the job they have to do. So in this chapter, we cover three themes. First, that the Village is led by Elders. Second, that the Elders must be wise, but the way we develop them means that they aren't always. And finally, we look at how Elders can gain the wisdom they need to lead.

Let's introduce the Elders.

The Elders

In public life, "The Elders," chaired by Kofi Annan, is an independent group of global leaders who work together for peace and human rights. The idea started with a conversation between entrepreneur Richard Branson and musician Peter Gabriel. The idea they discussed was simple: many communities look to their elders for guidance or to help resolve disputes. In an increasingly interdependent world—a global village—could a small, dedicated group of individuals use their collective experience and influence to help tackle some of the most pressing problems facing the world today? Richard Branson and Peter Gabriel took their idea of a group of global elders to Nelson Mandela, who agreed to support it. With the help of Graça Machel and Desmond Tutu, Mandela set about bringing the Elders together and formally launched the group in Johannesburg, July 2007. Their website tells us that the Elders aim to offer an independent voice, not bound by the interests of any nation, government, or institution and are committed to promoting the shared interests of humanity and universal human rights.

Elders are wise, experienced people to whom others can look for advice. Let's look at the role of Elders in business.

The Elders at Work

The Elders are a small number of very senior executives who sit alongside the CEO and together reach agreement about the strategic direction for the company. The Elders include the heads of the major business units, because success or failure in these large parts of the business can support or threaten the financial health of the whole. There may be leaders of the key functions, always finance, not always human resources. (Leaving HR off the team is puzzling. An organization is a collection of people pursuing a set of common goals. Why exclude the person responsible for making sure the organization has enough of the right people to achieve its strategic aims?) Finally, it may include some specialists or technical experts where these are part of the core capability of the business; for example, safety in the construction or extractive industries. Occasionally the group will co-opt members for short durations on specific topics.

The Elders tend to be a rich mix of the inherited and the imported, the ones the CEO trusts and wants to recruit as well as the sitting incumbents. The CEO is also an Elder, but in considering him or her as one of the Elders, we acknowledge that the CEO role goes much further. The executive team of Elders can number from roughly 5 to 20 people in size, depending on what we expect of them. A smaller team tends to be more tightly focused on strategy formulation and communication. A larger team is both harder to manage and less likely to be intimately involved in formulating the strategy because the goal of reaching agreement is harder with 20 people. It's not impossible, but more challenging.

Why would a CEO decide to work with a bigger advisory team? There could be several reasons. Maybe the CEO wants to keep potential disruptive influences in the room close and under observation. Perhaps it makes communicating across the whole organization easier, if functional heads together with the leaders of business units debate and conclude in the room together. Potentially, it could be to allow the CEO to scan all voices and keep an eye on talent as part of a succession planning process. It could even be to keep control—the CEO can act as a benevolent despot, because the chances of all 20 ganging up on him or her are slim.

What the CEO Inherits

Every new CEO casts a critical eye over the executive team that he or she inherits. There may be overlap with the CEO's own expertise, or gaps in the skills or capabilities needed to take the organization forward compared to what was needed in the past. There may be personality clashes with certain members. But the CEO doesn't have free rein to replace Elders at will; politics, vested interests, powerful heads of key business units, and existing relationships will all limit the capacity to act. One CEO said: "I changed some key people on my team—casualties help. I still have a couple of passengers, but you can't sack everyone and they can stay as long as they do no harm."

"Casualties"? It's a really symbolic act. Dismissing Elders reinforces the CEO's power but can also signal change in the organization—the discarded member may represent a part of the business that won't be important to the strategy in the future, or may be removed entirely from the strategy. And if that team member was disliked or generally seen as a poor role model, then moving that person on will bring real relief to employees.

And "passengers"? Everyone in the organization looks up to the top team, obviously to the CEO more than anyone else, but also to the executive team members. They are seen as powerful in their own right in addition to the power they have because they work so closely with the CEO and can put ideas into his or her head. Yet some of them may not be powerful at all, but passengers, safe in their position as long as they don't interfere or mess anything up. It's really a matter of pragmatism and politics. Pragmatism because the CEO needs to focus on getting the shape of the team broadly right, not exactly perfect—just make sure it works well enough. And politics, because these are powerful players and even if they lack or have lost their talent, they will have built networks and relationships, inside and outside the organization, that can make them hard to shift.

How Much Can Be Unpicked?

A CEO told the story about his tenure in the company. It is only since he felt he had been in the company long enough (by which he meant eight years in office) that he was able to freely form the executive team he wanted. That's a long time to wait! Corporate Elders are powerful and ambitious people, and they don't always play nicely, but they are part of the organizational fabric, and the CEO can't unpick too much in case it all unravels.

So some Elders are on the team because of their expertise, others for their unwavering support of the CEO, and still others for their ability to fix things. To be effective, the Elders need to be able to unite. They should look across and understand the whole business, not just their part of it, and act in the best interests of the majority. They have to set their prejudices, biases, and special interests to one side and act for the whole, for the sum of the parts. Just as in a traditional village, the Village Elders are critical in explaining the strategy to the other members of the Village to get their buy-in and ownership. If the Elders don't agree, can't act for the whole business, and don't feel committed to the cause, they won't get alignment from the Villagers, because their mixed messages will confound and confuse. But if they can align, then they will be able to lead execution effectively.

Unfortunately, the way organizations develop Elders has some key differences with how wise Elders grow in communities. They have age and experience in common. But it can be a struggle for corporate Elders to learn to care for the community as a whole. Let's turn next to our second theme and think about how Elders are developed at work and how big a transition they need to make to fill the Elder role with grace and dignity.

The Gamification of Leadership

The Elders face three challenges. The first is *gamification*, which is an ugly word for an important idea. It describes the use of game thinking to engage users and solve problems. Gamification techniques appeal to our natural desire for competition through making the rewards for accomplishing tasks visible to other players, or providing leader boards, as ways of encouraging players to compete. Unfortunately, gamification could also be used to describe aptly the talent and leadership development processes in many businesses. And the way we develop our leaders—through a competitive tournament—makes them ill-suited to the tasks of agreeing among themselves or of helping others to take charge of ideas.

It may not intentionally start out that way. But over time, the selection, development, and advancement of leaders typically resembles a kind of tournament. There are many good reasons for this. But there are also some negative consequences.

Gamification uses a process of competition to encourage people to find the best possible solution to a problem or to create the best new idea.[8] Unfortunately, what works with things (problem solving), rarely works as well with people (getting buy-in). The gamification of leadership produces leaders who are inclined to be combative and to compete, yet who need to collaborate and align. They default to command and control rather than to consult and influence.

Game On

If we look at the math of getting to the top in an organization, it's immediately apparent that only a tiny percentage of employees make it. *Forbes* reported in April 2012 that the largest 2,000 companies in the world produced $36 trillion in revenues and employed 83 million people, an average of 41,500 people each.[9] Assuming an average size of 10 for the executive team, that makes the Village Elders about 0.02 percent of the total population. How do you win a race like that? By competing—by being smarter, faster, more dedicated, or harder working than colleagues. It's a competitive model of promotion, and winners are distinguished from losers on five criteria: positive judgments about their work performance; early career success; less time spent at any one level of the organizational hierarchy compared with others; strong performance in previous competitions; and how fast the candidate has moved in the past (faster is better). It's literally described as a tournament, and as these executives progress up the hierarchy, they learn that competition works in getting them ahead.[10] They learn to compete to win personally more than they learn to collaborate to win as an organization. Individual, rather than team, reward systems often back this up.

IQ More Than EQ

The second challenge the Elders face is that they are just too smart. Executives have an average IQ of 125 or more, placing them in the top 3 percent of the population.[11] Businesses, like schools, encourage a strong focus on developing our intellectual muscle, on growing our intelligence to its maximum potential. And executives do need to be smarter than average to have the mental processing capacity to cut through the data overload. They need to be able to process data fast, separate the noise from the important information, and see the underlying themes and trends affecting their business. They need to be good at imagining future scenarios, picking the likeliest outcomes, and constructing a strategy to move ahead. These are all intellectual pursuits. Yet critically, they also need to be able to sell the strategy, to make it happen in practice. This requires a different kind of muscle. It demands our EQ—our emotional intelligence.[12]

At one level, EQ is about empathy because persuading other people to align with you means getting inside their heads and understanding them and their needs. Intimacy matters. But EQ is more than empathy and social insight. Sometimes it can take extraordinary self-control to work productively with someone who adds great value, but whose approach and ideas may be very different from our own. One CEO spoke of walking and talking with a colleague, with a smile on his face, but with his hands clenched and stuffed deep into his trouser pockets, because he was so angry with how the colleague was approaching a situation. EQ is as much about self-control as it is about building good relationships with others.

IQ helps us to see and analyze the strategic picture, to make decisions faster, and to grasp the business better. In our experience this is well honed in senior executives, while EQ is frequently underdeveloped and is exercised less.

Solace in Expertise

It's an uncertain world at the top of an organization. The job of the Village Elders is to ensure the long-term survival of the organization, and this means trying to read the future. The path ahead is indistinct at best, and we are trying to map a way forward into the unknown. The first time we try something new, it's unclear how it will turn out. Experimenting to stay ahead of the competition is important, but it also means making decisions with incomplete information. What worked before may not work again so a lot of our time is spent in unknown territory, as we grapple with new ideas and pilot new approaches. In addition, an executive who built his or her reputation on a particular expertise (manufacturing, branding, production, systems' engineering, finance, distribution, human resources) now needs to understand how all these specialities operate in unison in order to make the business work. It's not enough to remain an expert. This is why the MBA is such a popular degree globally, because it teaches all of these disciplines and then explains how they interact to form a business.

Overdoing It

The Elders' third challenge in doing a good job of leading strategy execution is to learn to influence, not to do. In any transition, the temptation is to keep doing our old job. We are familiar with it, and we probably got promoted because we were good at it. So it's an escape hatch from the uncertainties we face in our new job and an opportunity to keep our self-confidence high by dipping back into the comfort zone of the job we used to do.

It won't work. Meddling with the old job in marketing, when the Elder job specification calls for strategic leadership of the whole business, is plain unacceptable. It's tough for the Elder to step back and guide rather than act, to remember and feel comfortable that it's the Village members who execute the strategy.

This transition is the most challenging because the job is very strategic, and it's hard to contemplate a job that requires lots of enabling, with all that comforting "doing" now delegated to someone else. And it's not even straightforward delegation, because the job is more about selling ideas. Our leadership believability is being tested. Can we persuade them or not? Can we win their hearts and minds rather than simply tell them what to do?

A Diplomatic Tale

Sir Jeremy Greenstock was a career diplomat from 1969 to 2004. He served as political director in London from 1996 to 1998, as U.K. ambassador to the UN in New York from 1998 to 2003 and as U.K. special envoy for Iraq, based in Baghdad from 2003 to 2004. Today he is chairman of the UN Association in the UK and chairman of the strategic advisory company Gatehouse Advisory Partners Ltd.

Greenstock talks about what he learned as U.K. ambassador to the UN in New York:

> *The context was complex and the UN was very busy. The U.K. Mission was involved in everything, yet there were only a dozen of us. I had to let the desk officers take tactics and negotiations as far as they possibly could without supervision, or I would have limited what could be achieved. I delegated to the maximum, while accepting responsibility for any mistakes. As a result they started developing and so could take on even more independently. There is something truly satisfying in creating the capacity for competent individuals to use their talent to its limit all day long. Of course, this takes personal confidence on both sides.*[13]

Some aspects of the job, such as too few staff and too much to do, supported and forced Greenstock to strategize and let others get on with the doing. And it's a fine balance, which is another reason it can be challenging. Give people too much leeway, and they may be incompetent and feel afraid or overloaded. Give them too little freedom, and they will feel that they are being micromanaged and have no stake in the outcome. People need to be stretched but not overstretched. The first step is to start to let go.

The Elder Is Uniquely Ill-Qualified for the Job

So where does all this leave us? To summarize, the very promotion system that gets senior executives to the top makes them uniquely ill-equipped to do the very different job required of them once they are at the top. Having arrived in the top job by being competitive, smarter than average, and reliably delivering results, they now need to collaborate for the good of the whole enterprise and to work with their emotional intelligence to persuade equally smart people to execute the chosen strategy. They need to be able to see and understand how the business works, to think about how the whole system operates (not just a specialist or functional part of the whole), and to encourage the organization to align, collaborate, and pull together. These are not the skills that got them the job in the first place and it's a steep learning curve.

We need collaborative Elders who can empathize with the fear that change can breed and encourage others to action despite the uncertainty, yet that's not how we groom our leaders to succeed. The bottom line is that we need to change the way we develop and grow people so that they are not just credible experts but also believable leaders by the time they reach the giddy heights of this 0.02 percent job.

Credible and Believable Leaders

We need to develop leaders who are both credible and believable. Credibility lies in a leader's expertise in interpreting and giving direction to solve knotty problems. It's the ability to construct a logical story about why things have to change that makes sense. It's a deep and rich capability. Believability is complementary but different. Believability means that others see the leader's actions and values as genuine and principled, and the leader as a trusted and inspirational guide to be followed. Credibility is followers' certainty that your decisions are good, that you know what you are doing. Believability is confidence in your values so that you are trusted to act in the right way. To be authentic, the leader needs both. Credible leaders can fail because they cannot build conviction even though their logic is indisputable. Equally and dangerously, believable leaders can destroy organizations because they are plausible even though they may be misguided.

Leaders need to know what they are doing and also be able to sell it convincingly. It's a tough transition and not all make it. What to do?

The transition to Elder is probably the biggest there is—from expert to generalist, from fact-based decisions to judgments based on a blend of experience and instinct, from functional certainty to cross-functional collaboration and enabling others rather than doing it yourself. This reminds us of Marshall Goldsmith's book— *What Got You Here Won't Get You There*.[14]

At this level, it's hard to distinguish between a failed transition and someone who simply fell foul of the politics. Yves Doz, an emeritus professor at INSEAD business school, describes leadership unity as one aspect of strategic agility, meaning the ability of the top team to make decisions fast, without getting bogged down in win-lose politics. Politics happen. Executive search firms don't always get the opportunity to watch the executive team before recommending an outside hire, and sometimes the newcomer just doesn't fit well into the existing team.

It's more visible when a CEO fails to transition well into the job. A *Harvard Business Review* article in 2000 looked at CEO churn, with CEOs appointed after 1985 three times more likely to be fired than those appointed before that date.[15] We attribute this churn largely to choosing leaders who are good technically but who lack the leadership skills "to move the human heart." The Center for Creative Leadership has also undertaken research into derailment; that is, when a formerly successful executive with a good performance track record plateaus, is demoted, or is fired. They find four major causes, three personal (inability to adapt, inability to build and lead a team, and problems with interpersonal relationships) and one business (failure to meet business objectives).[16] It's the same conclusion as ours—the failure is more to do with underdeveloped personal leadership skills than business mistakes.

So all three aspects of this transition to the executive team of Elders; collaboration (rather than competition); EQ (moving the human heart and interpersonal relationships); and empowerment (building and leading teams) are critical.

Elders Behaving Badly Have to Go

Many of the CEOs we interviewed had stories about challenges they had faced with their executive teams, or some members of the teams. We heard earlier from Irene Dorner, the president and CEO of HSBC USA, where she told us of her belief that not to understand the strategy is a flaw. She goes further: "Not knowing the strategy is a serious flaw. But to know the strategy and to disagree with it is a fatal flaw. I have zero tolerance—if they do harm, they have to go."

This quote is a lively illustration of research done in the 1990s on the importance of complete ownership of the strategy by the senior team.[17] The CEO can't transform an organization on his or her own, but needs the support of a "guiding coalition"—a strong set of peers on the executive team. If one of these executives, with considerable authority, disagrees with the strategy, then he or she needs to go. It's a fatal flaw. If the executive doesn't see the same challenges and opportunities as colleagues, then messages communicated from this most senior team become garbled. It's downright dangerous to tolerate dissent among the Elders. Debate, naturally. But once agreement has been reached and the strategy announced, the time for debate has passed. Continued debate at this stage is too late and turns into disagreement and even subversion of what you are trying to achieve. As Dorner says, the only policy is one of zero tolerance.

Disagreement is not always overt. How do you spot when someone is only paying lip service to the strategy, but not backing it for real? It's the law of unintended outcomes; when something doesn't move forward as planned, follow the detail and you will find the root cause. Dorner again: "My cat suddenly started behaving strangely at the age of 6; begging for food and trying to raid the fridge. I found out that my stepson had been feeding the cat, hence its change in behavior. It's the same when somebody doesn't follow or actively subverts the strategy; follow the detail and you find out why." So we need to be alert and look out for actions, decisions. and activities that we didn't expect. These are all clues that something is out of kilter. Then we need to keep looking until we find the root cause.

Or Can You Get Them Across the Line?

Jeremy Pelczer, chairman of WaterAid, was previously president and CEO of American Water from September 2003 to December 2005. His executive team of 10 people led a Village of 80 (out of a total of 8,000 employees) when he was CEO. During his tenure, he led a new strategy, including a culture change program to embrace change and adopt a more dynamic business language. Pelczer knew that he had to get his 10 Village Elders to buy in first: "I held meetings with my executive team of 10, with a professional facilitator to help me to deal with individuals' issues and get them across the line. The facilitator was robust and challenging, using direct language about the need to be aligned. He'd say things like 'Up periscope guys, you need to see the big picture.' There was no way we could launch the strategy until we were in complete alignment."[18]

Pelczer's message is clear. Work with members of the executive team to give them a chance to overcome their fatal flaw before you ask them to leave. Don't expect all the members of your executive team to buy into changes immediately or at the same time. Some will need to be persuaded or, as Pelczer puts it, to be moved "across the line." More importantly, only when the most senior team is in agreement and on message can the change process safely start. Don't launch before the Elders are onside, or the fault lines will spread and grow further down the organization.

Keep Thinking Ahead

After the strategy launch at American Water, the executive team task became to review progress. Pelczer adds: "It was important to set specific time aside in the one day business performance reviews to focus on strategy, or the whole meeting would have defaulted to operations. The reviews importantly included the process of buy-in." Again, clear advice. Focus on reviewing progress toward achieving the strategy. Don't get distracted by the ever-present temptation to default to conversations around tactics or to start meddling in execution. Lift your sights and make sure that you are on track with the bigger, overarching goal. Even more than that, in addition to paying attention to business results, also measure whether employee buy-in is growing and spreading. Here is the echo of Levin's advice earlier, with his employee surveys. You are checking that your leaders of execution are motivated and engaged and inspiring others.

A good executive team is focused on the long-term survival of the company. Its job is to think ahead with the CEO, so the team members will suggest or make decisions that may look less than optimal in the short term, but that will add value in the longer term. Alignment among the Elders is important because they need to be robust in defending decisions that may be challenged because they make less sense to others who lack their helicopter view. A good team also provides thought leadership and challenge. Members are critical to execution, because if they cannot agree on what needs to be done for the long-term survival of the enterprise and if they disagree and operate along functional or business unit lines, then these schisms will be exacerbated and exaggerated by the Village members themselves. If the bosses are fighting, we will also need to fight one level down. If the Elders are aligned but then fail to communicate effectively, the layers of employees below them will still be muddled and confused. It is critical for strategy execution to get the right people on the executive team, acting in the right way.

This small top executive layer can enable or disable others to or from action and execution. So we need them to get them on board with the strategy and then have them focus on selling it to others. They need to live up to their title of Elders. They need to be wise.

Let's turn to the third theme of the chapter and walk through how to help them, step by step.

Building Wise Elders

The Village Elders are not a team. In fact, the "top team" is a misnomer. It is not a team at all. This may seem like a strange statement, but it really isn't. Think of it as a simple observation based on years of experience of working with senior executives. Teams can bring great advantages to a business when the members work well together and generally make better decisions than individual team members on their own.[19] Team-building is a worthwhile and powerful activity. It helps clarify roles, responsibilities, and accountabilities; it encourages collaboration; it argues for focus on a common goal. Team-building is pursued at all levels in an organization, and high-performing teams are the prize we seek.

When Is a Team Not a Team?

Although we often talk about, or refer to, the top team, the Village Elders are not a team in the usual sense of the word. This is because the Elders are the most powerful players in the business. Each one could, or thinks he or she could, take the CEO position. The tournament model means that, while they work together, the Elders are simultaneously in the final rounds of the competition for the ultimate prize—the top job. This is why, when one of them succeeds to the CEO spot, it's most likely that the major contenders will leave to find the top job somewhere else. They have lost this tournament, so they move on to another. Think about what happened when Andrew Mackenzie lost out to Tom Albanese for the CEO position at Rio Tinto in 2007. Mackenzie left to join the rival BHP Billiton, where he became CEO in May 2013. In contrast with the openness and transparency that characterizes team-building, there are conspiracies, coalitions, and bilateral deals at the top. There has to be mutual respect and give and take for anything to work. There may be an unwillingness to confront, or an over-willingness to confront. It can become extreme. We worked with one executive team where two members had a long-standing feud, to the extent that they refused to be in the same room as each other. Power imbalances can lead some Elders to keep quiet when they should speak up, or sometimes not to speak at all.

Getting mutual respect among the members of the executive team should be counted as success, however little teamwork may actually take place. If there is respect in the room, at least there will be debate and give and take. Everyone will bring their expertise to problem solving and will leave the room with truly agreed-upon direction and supporting actions, even if the disagreements and trade-offs en route have been messy.

A Virtuous Circle

If we can't get the Village Elders right, the company's strategy will never be executed. Instead, we'll be watching infighting and politics at the top—not a great spectator sport when long-term survival is at stake. How can we develop a group of colleagues who can work effectively together and agree and align, at least publicly, on what needs to be done? How can we gather the Elders? It's about being clear about the strategy, achieving consensus around tight business objectives linked to the strategy, having the challenging conversations needed to reach consensus, and instilling good governance procedures. We are trying to create a virtuous circle of loyal and confident Villagers who are able to follow the Elders in a way that in turn makes the Elders better leaders.

First let's think about the different leadership that the Elders need to display, based on the kind of strategy they may be pursuing.

Be Clear About the Kind of Strategy

David Levin, the CEO of UBM, says it's a good idea to start execution with being clear about the kind of strategy you are pursuing. He takes a fresh look at strategy using a health analogy and distinguishes between chronic illness and chronic wellness, each bringing its own challenges.

Chronic illness is hard to deal with. It occurs when a line of business is in slow but steady decline, like the print or magazine business. Levin says: "Managing a retreat is really the hardest thing in business—how do you transmit the message and get people to move faster and do more?"[20] It's a challenge to keep morale and motivation high in a group of people who are essentially presiding over their own demise. What is the incentive for them to speed up toward the end? Levin recommends transparency, complete honesty, and a common language concerning what needs to happen. The trick is to keep focused on a business goal, albeit the goal happens to be eventual closure. Don't pretend everything is all right, because people are smart and they understand the truth and respect being treated like adults who can be trusted with the truth. At the same time, don't let despondency and despair set in. The end of the business, properly led, can still bring good financial returns on the road to the end. Also, the end of the business doesn't necessarily mean the end of the people, if resources can be reallocated to more successful parts of the business.

Chronic wellness strangely also brings problems. In this situation, the business is growing, and so everyone should be happy and investment should flow toward these high performing stars.[21] Levin's advice here is: "Arrogance, hubris and comfortable groupthink are the classic risks. You have to ensure diversity, so you stop people getting too comfortable and becoming too predictable while exploiting the opportunity." The challenge is almost the opposite of that with chronic illness, in that here, morale and motivation can be so high that overoptimism takes us down the tricky road of excess and overinvestment. So the messages from the executive team need to be quite different. It's about common sense and prudence.

Levin adds a third option, continuing with the medical theme, of a more acute nature—surgery. In this case, pieces need to be grafted on or removed, so we enter the world of mergers and acquisitions and divestments in order to get the portfolio right. The task of integrating a new acquisition, or the job of readying a part of the business for profitable sale, is different again from chronic illness or wellness.

We couldn't resist adding a fourth category to Levin's three.[22] This is trauma, another version of acute illness, but less predictable and more extreme. This is the unexpected disaster, for example,

Johnson & Johnson recalling Tylenol in 1982 after some packets were laced with potassium cyanide and seven people died. The 2010 Deepwater Horizon oil spill in the Gulf of Mexico on the BP-operated Macondo Prospect is another sad example. The rig exploded and then sank, claiming 11 lives. A sea-floor oil gusher flowed for 87 days before it was successfully capped, leading to the largest accidental marine spill in the history of the industry. Criminal and civil settlements cost BP over $40 billion by early 2013. However vigilant the leadership is, sometimes terrible accidents happen, and they're big enough to be a threat to the health of the whole business. Under these circumstances, the leaders need to move quickly and without panic.

The four types of strategy have four matching leadership styles. Chronic illness needs transparency, honesty, clear targets, and compassion; chronic wellness needs to remove too much ebullience from the system and hold steady; surgery needs strong relationship skills to integrate purchases and sell units; and trauma needs calm but speedy reactions.

This isn't a book about strategy, and the aim isn't to add a new strategy model to the dozens already on the market. Whichever strategy model we are following, the message is the same. When gathering the Elders, we need to be clear about the kind of strategy we are pursuing so that we know what kind of performance we expect from them. Larger organizations are likely to be pursuing a combination of strategies, so the executive team has to be versatile. Its members should give different messages and offer different leadership approaches to separate parts of the business as they exhort different strategies.

We need the Elders to agree the strategy and then to agree how to pursue the strategy. Is this possible?

Consensus

There is a series of cartoons by three-time Pulitzer Prize–winning editorial cartoonist Jeff MacNelly that includes a picture and a description of consensus that is pretty accurate: a shy creature, often sought but seldom found.[23] The trouble is that the world is a complex place for people to navigate. Organizations are big; indeed some are huge: the U.S. Department of Defense employs over 3 million people, the U.S.-based global store Walmart and the People's Liberation Army of China both employ over 2 million. The U.K. National Health Service and McDonald's (as the largest private sector company) both nearly reach 2 million employees.[24] Big organizations are laden with politics and complexity. Even when we're not at work, we are bombarded with a constant cacophony of noise—24/7 news reports, e-mails, tweets, blogs, and other social media. And in the middle of all this, what we need most is the ability to cut through all the white noise and make sense of it. So consensus may be a rare beast, but we need the Elders to hunt it down. And as Martin Luther King suggested, the CEO will have to help mold it.

Amid this noise and complexity, we are asking our senior executive team members to be very clear about what they are asking us to do. If they are unclear with us, it's very easy to find things to do. Activity is not a challenge. There is always more on the to-do list than can be done. It's determining where we should be focusing our effort that is the challenge. We need to be focused on business—what our business really needs to prosper—not busyness. What does "busyness" mean? It means that people will be spread too thinly. They will be trying to hedge their bets and do too much. In attempting to do everything, the very real danger is that they will achieve nothing. So we are demanding that our executive team align around the critical activities that will move our business forward.

The Village Elders must agree to prioritize the five big strategic things that they believe we should achieve. Strategy is essentially a combination of choosing among future scenarios and then deciding upon the key activities needed to achieve the favored scenario. It's about setting a few key targets to create the future you have decided you want. If we fail to prioritize or if we compromise and agree to do too much, the result will be confusion and busyness in the organization. If we fudge the key strategic conversation in the executive team, we will pay for it in dissipated energy and lack of execution.

A Battle for Focus

We heard before from Jeremy Pelczer, the former president and CEO of American Water and now chairman of WaterAid. He explains the battle for focus like this: "The CEO needs energy and presence to get agreement on the 3–5 priorities; 3–5 'must win' battles. It's a bloody fight to get these to be agreed upon. If everything is a priority, then nothing is."[25] Pelczer is arguing for absolute focus on a handful of strategic priorities.

It was the same story at IBM when Lou Gerstner joined as CEO in 1993. In 1990, IBM was the second most profitable company in the world. Then from 1991 to 1993, it lost nearly $16 billion, and the stock plummeted. Tony O'Driscoll was performance architecture lead at IBM in 2007. In this role, he led the development of breakthrough performance analysis techniques to drive sales productivity and performance. He recalls his time at IBM: "I can still remember the three things Lou asked us to focus on, even today, without notes in front of me. He said we had to unlock the knowledge in the brains of our people; to change our mindset to computing, not computers; and we had to go to market as one IBM. A lot has been written about this in the press, but those three focus areas undergirded the whole transformation. I can tell you, I was there, and Armonk was reeling that day."[26] Gerstner believed that the business model had to change—from selling computers to advising about computing and selling packages that included others' products in addition to IBM's hardware.[27] It was the precursor to IBM's move into the service business. All technical details aside, here were three strategic imperatives to guide execution through the life of his tenure. Simple, clear, and direct enough to be recalled, without notes, 20 years later. That's how Gerstner turned IBM around.

If we ask people to focus on more than a few key strategic activities, we are going to get a muddle of busyness. If we can't simplify, we will end up with a proliferation of initiatives and will be trying to do too much. The wider our spread and reach, the more opportunities we give people who don't want to play, the opportunity to snipe. Fudging conversations brings superficial buy-in but leads to disastrous consequences for execution, because different individuals will believe that they have signed up for different things. Disagreement among the top few, whether fundamental or imagined, will kill our capability for execution. We need one voice.

The Elders have to be aligned. They have no choice; it's their job. The targets must be simple, they must be few, and they must be sold with conviction. If there are cracks among the Elders, they will become ravines by the time they reach the Village, and the Villagers will be shouting at each other across the gaps. They will hardly be able to hear each other, and they certainly won't agree on how to cross the divide. Don't expect agreement to be easy. The CEO's role is critical here in pushing, shoving, and cajoling until real agreement is achieved.

Whatever their capability, however much they add or detract from the quality of strategic conversation, there is one qualification that all Elders must have. They must back the CEO in word and action on the chosen strategy. They may not achieve real consensus in the closed debating chamber of the strategy planning session—there may be some trade-offs and compromises—but the rest of the world needs to see consensus from them.

Real agreement is more than a "form of words" that keeps everyone onside. It means a solid sense of the future, a determination to refuse compromise and seek synergy. To achieve this elusive consensus, we may need some hard conversations.

Agree to Disagree

If the Elders vie for power and attention, if they compete for resources rather than think about what is best for the whole company, then what looks like good and thoughtful strategic debate may in reality be the expression of partisan interests designed to win more resources than colleagues. An Elder should expect to be, at some stage, at odds with fellow Elders. This is a good thing. The executive team that finds agreement too easily is likely to lack imagination, or the will and determination to push through to a harder but better decision, or the zest for debate. Team members will become a conspiracy and collude in mediocrity. What we need is a process that allows us to engage in hard debate and still work productively together once a decision is reached.

It's time for the whole team to confront challenging issues. There are various phrases for this around the world. Indians talk of the elephant in the room, while Canadians prefer the moose on the table, and Australians worry about the koala in the chair. They are all metaphors for the same thing—an inability to talk about what really matters or an ability to skirt important issues. Everyone knows that there's an elephant in the room, but we tread lightly and carefully around it, terrified to wake it. Real debate is central to the capability of the executive team to create a viable strategy and, even more importantly, to commit to its execution. The aim of authentic debate is to argue it through until everyone believes in the solution and is heartily committed to it. If people pretend or go along with it for an easier life, then later they will either comply (I'll do as much as I am told but only as long as you watch me carefully) or subvert the decision (I will pretend to play along, but I'll undermine whatever I can, whenever I can).[28]

Faking It

Why would people pretend to agree, rather than speak up? Why would they go along with a decision, but in reality give grudging compliance, or even work secretly to undermine what appeared to be a group decision? We are talking about serious professionals at or near the top of their game who are paid large sums of money to shepherd the organization safely forward. Why would they not speak up in adult conversation?

There are many reasons. Maybe it's near the end of the tournament, and so the stakes on winning and losing the CEO title are at their highest. They may keep silent to win the popular vote. Or it may not feel safe to declare their honest opinion. When politics are rife, you play the game and you want to win. Sometimes they are just plain scared. There are strong egos at all levels in an organization, and they are at their most pressured, and pressurizing, at the top. There is a tacit hierarchy in the executive committee among a group of apparent peers. It's always worth asking the question, "What does silence mean?" When someone doesn't speak, is it because they agree, but don't feel the need to say so? What else might be going on?

We need a process to legitimize challenge.

Red-Flag Conversations

The meeting room was oak-panelled. On one side of the room were miniature flags of the world, representing physical locations of the company. As he entered the room, one executive picked up one of the country flags and, without a word, put the flag in front of him on the table. A colleague asked what the flag was for. He answered: "At some point in this meeting I am going to say something that you are not going to want to hear. Before I speak, I am going to hold up the flag so that you can be prepared for what is coming next." He cleverly prepared the room for debate and depersonalized the issue at the same time. Everyone looked at the flag, not at him. Sure enough, at one point in the meeting he fulfilled his promise and waved the flag before he made a contentious point. By the end of the meeting, three others had walked across the room and picked up the flag before they spoke. By the next meeting, it had already been accepted as the norm.

Theirs was a country flag, but let's think of it as a red flag.[29] A red flag is commonly used all over the world, by the armed forces, shipping, railways, and others to denote "beware, danger, look out." As an international symbol its meaning should be recognized by executives everywhere. When strategy is debated, there are serious issues at stake, core to the future survival and prosperity of an organization, so emotions can run high. The tournament model leads naturally to a desire to win, and unless monitored, sometimes the debate gets personal. The trick is to remove the threat of confrontation by focusing on the issue, not the person. The red flag is a way to signal what's coming and to keep debate focused on the topic. Choose any symbol you like to enable red-flag conversations. And keep it human. Here's a very simple litmus test. Are people joking and laughing at times, as well as being involved in constructive challenge at others? It makes the atmosphere better, less intense, and more enjoyable. We're not advising humor as a diversionary tactic or as a disguised means of attack, but as true warmth and connection among colleagues.

Don't Go into Politics

Politics are a natural part of life, as human beings navigate their way through complex situations and relationships. At their most subtle, a partial disclosure of facts or a call on a friend to whisper into the ear of another friend is simple social lubrication—a way to keep the world going around without too much upset. At their most deadly, they are Politics with a capital P, which suggests manipulation and dirty tricks. We know one former CEO who was successfully ousted, three years ahead of time and way too soon in the succession planning process, by a potential successor. Now that's Politics—an individual out for him- or herself, with the good of the whole enterprise coming in a distant second. (By the way, although the maneuver was successful in removing the CEO, it backfired on the perpetrator, who was taken off the succession list immediately. But he was not removed from the company. He was too powerful and too good an operator.)

How can we spot and deal with Politics? Irene Dorner at HSBC gave us Dorner's Law of Unintended Consequences, which is a good starting place: look out for people who promise to adjust but seem to be taking an inordinate amount of time. Also watch for unexpected events or outcomes. One CEO recalls the moment when he spotted Politics. "It became increasingly clear that a colleague was having conversations different to those he alleged he was having. He was still networking with the old guard and with other stakeholders outside of the company. His political networking was intended to sow seeds of doubt among the newly recruited leaders and those still sitting on the fence. He was trying to build a network of allies to confuse the evidence and implicate others in the mistakes of the past. He had to go." Dorner's Law of Zero Tolerance.

Political influence will always affect organizational outcomes, in the same way that bacteria help to develop healthy immune systems. Kept in balance, politics will live inside the organization as a social lubricant and be kept in check through good disciplines and behavior. The real problem comes when political behavior develops to a level where it begins to infect the systems and the people within them. Then you need to get rid of the source of infection.

Where are we now with the Elders? The type of strategy is clear, whether chronic illness or wellness, and with the leadership style adjusted to fit. We have debated our way through to real consensus on three to five key strategic objectives, with no Political hidden agendas. By now, we think our Elders are wise.

The last piece of the puzzle is to make sure the arrangement is robust and not dependent on the personalities currently in the room. In addition to wise Elders, we need good governance procedures for the wisdom to endure.

Good Governance

The executive team leads governance and compliance: every organization must operate within the law. Governance is a big topic. What exactly is it? At one level it is legal compliance and a healthy code of ethics. But it is also about the simple rhythm of how things run on a daily basis. There are plenty of corporate guidelines on the legal and philosophical aspects of governance. Here we suggest some practical, simple, good organizational routines and daily practices. Good governance is the drumbeat behind execution.

Every organization has lots of meetings, and some important ones are held regularly, like executive team meetings or functional team meetings. Why not hold important, decision-making management team meetings on the same day of each month? In that way, people can move from one meeting to the next without losing focus or forgetting information en route. If you are a key player on many teams, it will make it a long day; for example, to start with the executive team meeting, then move to a functional meeting, then on to a communications meeting, and so on. On the upside, the meetings should take less time than they used to. When consecutive meetings are held on the same day, we can remember the information we just heard that now needs to be communicated to the next team meeting, rather than having to be reminded about what was said at a meeting days or weeks ago. As meetings cascade over the day, some information can recorded in a document, without needing to be read or to be presented again, because everyone will have heard it in some form at a previous meeting. The alternative process, of meetings scattered over the month, means that critical information has to be recalled and recounted several times. When you think about it, it's a real waste of time. It also becomes more of an effort to track follow-through.

Put It in the Diary

Schedule important meetings 12 months in advance and stick to the schedule. If meetings are arranged at short notice or if the dates keep changing, then people won't take them as seriously—because if they were important, they would be immovable in the calendar. Also, if the dates keep changing, it is unlikely that the principals will be able to change their diaries at short notice to match the new schedule and so will send deputies instead. Deputies may not all have decision-making authority, and this will lead to rework as the same items will need to be put back on the agenda for a final decision at another meeting. Again, a real time-waster.

The third piece is to make sure that everyone knows who is responsible and accountable for what, to clarify roles and to put an escalation procedure in place. If something cannot be decided or resolved, then it should be very clear where the knotty problem needs to go next in order to be dealt with. A lot of decisions aren't made simply because they move around the organization waiting to find the right person with the authority to decide. Sometimes, it can be a long wait.

The last piece of fundamental governance is to stick to good meeting rules. Read relevant papers beforehand (unless you work for Amazon, see the story in the next paragraph) and come prepared. The task of the meeting is to raise issues, make decisions, institute actions, and follow up on them—not to exchange information that can be read in advance. People will join in more freely and have more fun if they are better informed. And try to ditch the dreadful habit of meetings that last exactly one hour. There are already too many meetings in most organizations, and to finish the 10 a.m. meeting at 11 a.m. and then arrive simultaneously as the next meeting starts at 11 a.m. is physically impossible, unless you are Hermione Granger.[30] What's wrong with 45-minute meetings?

Lou Gerstner changed the way meetings ran at IBM. When he joined as CEO in 1993, he did two unexpected things. The first was to attend the whole of a three-day customer conference, rather than just making a token appearance—thus signaling to IBM'ers the importance of customers. The second was to send an internal memo to all leaders saying he didn't want any more long PowerPoint presentations at meetings. Instead he wanted two letters; the first on the business and how it was running and the second on recommendations to grow it in the future. Before Gerstner, the expectation was to spend the day before a meeting polishing the PowerPoint deck in preparation for pitching ideas at the meeting. This edict from Gerstner saved a whole lot of polishing time and moved the conversation at the meeting from pitching to debate and decisions. Jeff Bezos, the founder and CEO of Amazon, does something very similar. His policy is that those who call a meeting must provide a three-page briefing on the objective of the meeting and the content for discussion. In a one-hour meeting, everyone spends 20 minutes reading the note and then 40 minutes debating the decision.

As Mark Twain said, "It usually takes me more than three weeks to prepare a good impromptu speech." To be able to get complex ideas down to a note that can be read in 20 minutes takes discipline and thoughtfulness.

We have almost reached the end of the journey to wisdom. Our Elders are now capable of authentic debate and can agree among themselves on a handful of strategic objectives to guide the Village in strategy execution. They are credible and believable leaders, worthy of following. The final step in their journey toward wisdom is to make sure that they are well followed.

Build Confidence in the Village

The top 100 Village needs confidence to push back on the Elders and to tell the story of what's really going on in the organization. Sometimes it will be bad news, but if the Village hides the truth, for whatever reason, then the top team will be driving blind. Its members won't know how the strategy is working out in practice. The critical piece for the Elders is to make the hardest transition of all—from ownership to leadership.

Ownership means that it's your possession, to hold or to pass to others, as you see fit. Leadership means that you want the Village to feel ownership and to take responsibility for action. It's yours to lead and theirs to do. The Elders' task is to inspire, not to tell the Villagers what to do. Tell them how to be, by evoking the principles and values of the organization. Be guardians of the culture, the way to do things, rather than the nitty-gritty of the action item list. Help the Villagers to think through the right attitude and outlook. We talk in Chapter 1 about the importance of voice in helping people feel real ownership. The Villagers need to believe that their opinions count, in order for them to step forward and take ownership for action. The Elders need to listen to them, not talk at them.

The Elders' challenge is to avoid intimidating the Villagers into compliance, because they are afraid that they might not be as smart or cannot see as far ahead. Elders cannot show frustration if the Villagers can't see or get it as clearly or as quickly as them. The prime directive[31] is to help them. So the key execution question for the Elders is how to use their leadership credibility and believability to sell ideas to the Villagers and to guide and applaud as they move to action.

A Real Elder

The Senior Executive Program at London Business School elects a class representative to act as an interface between the faculty and staff members of the school and the class members. Usually, the representative gets very busy, running around organizing events and meetings. One time, the class voted in a middle-aged African woman as its representative. She delegated everything, working with about a third of the class to generate a hive of activity, with the Queen Bee looking relaxed and colorful in its midst. The class got a lot more done during her tenure than it had during the tenure of others. She said, "If I'm the leader, that means I don't need to do it myself." If you're reading this and you're an Elder, relax, you've made it. If you work for an Elder, help the Elder to stop getting his or her hands dirty.

Summary

In this chapter we look critically at the role of the Village Elders, or the CEO and executive team. We identify who the Elders are and then look at the three aspects that can stop them from being as effective as they might be once they transition into this very senior role. Specifically, they are challenged by a leadership development process that teaches them to compete, to value their intellect more than their emotional intelligence, and to keep on doing the job themselves instead of spending more of their time thinking about how the job should be done and supporting others in action. In short, they transition into a position for which they appear to be uniquely ill-qualified. The transition challenges are the biggest they have ever faced.

We then consider specific ways to develop Elders to be highly effective in leading strategy execution. The Elders need clarity about the kind of strategy they are advocating and the ability to agree to focus on no more than five strategic imperatives. They need to learn how to debate constructively in order to decide fundamentally on this limited number of imperatives and to adopt good practices for effective and efficient governance.

Last, the Elders need to build the top 100 Village into confident and competent followers who can own and lead strategy execution. It's a virtuous circle—good followers make good leaders, and vice versa.

We cover the key skills in inspiring others to action in the next chapter, "Power Up Feeling."

3

Power Up Feeling

Don't believe them when they tell you it's not personal. I spend ten
hours at work a day. It's deeply personal.
—Pramod Bhasin[1]

Aristotle and Euripides

Aristotle is the father of modern science, the first person to clas-
sify areas of human knowledge into distinct disciplines such as
mathematics, biology, and ethics. Some of these classifications are
still used today. He is the father of logic and reasoning. Euripides,
in contrast, was a poet and prolific playwright who went against
the trend of the day in the fourth century BC by portraying slaves
as intelligent and women as strong. He focused on the inner lives
and motives of his characters, which was new to Greek audiences
of the day. Aristotle or Euripides? Today's leader needs both.
This chapter isn't making the case for leaders to overemote. But
it is making the argument for using more of a capability that is
underdeveloped in many leaders today. We need to harness the
power of emotion.

I Don't Believe You

"His face was red, contorted with real anger but still controlled.
He wasn't looking at me but through me. His workmates stopped
what they were doing to watch. It was now an amphitheater down
in the bowels of the factory. 'Most of the problems 'round here are

wearing ties,' he hissed. I felt a little overdressed for the continuing conversation. 'You and your mates up there have well and truly mucked it up this time.'

"The strategy was good. As a leadership team we had taken great care and it was built on detailed market research, extensive customer interviews and broad stakeholder agreement. The new strategy brought with it a challenging change program, it meant re-engineering the whole business, but pilot studies had given us confidence that we were on the right track. The new structure displaced the old silos and flattened them into an integrated and streamlined customer-centric structure. Three layers of management were taken out and we were pushing decision making close to the factory floor through continuous improvement teams.

"This man was angry because his work routines had been upturned and he had a new team leader. He was being asked to do different work. He was being trained and encouraged to take on a more influential decision making role but he saw that as 'being asked to take on a manager's job.'

"This is where the conversations get very real.

"For this man, strategies were stories made up by people who didn't understand what real work felt like, working hierarchically and geographically a long way from where he stood. He just wanted to do a good job, and not be fussed by all this noise. He was frustrated by the inefficiency of learning. His anxiety built into resentment and then into rejection and that's what he wanted to vent."

This graphic story from a CEO leading a transformation program in a manufacturing facility demonstrates the real pressure that strategy execution places on people. This employee's language wasn't as polite as we have reported, and his demeanor was threatening. This CEO is one of the braver ones. He wanted to get out and find out for real how people were coping with all the changes, and this man was ready to tell him. For him, there were too many parts moving simultaneously. New boss, new working practices, new responsibilities, the mess of everyone learning new things at the same time. And as for that lovely word, "empowerment," which is used to encourage people who can't delegate to let go of all the control? Well, frankly, he didn't want any of it.

This is the stark reality of strategy execution. It stirs up feelings. More Euripides than Aristotle.

Getting to the Top

What does it take to make it to a senior executive position in an organization? As we have seen, IQ ranks pretty high on the short list of qualifications. Raw intelligence does matter. Senior leaders need to be able to cope with vast amounts of information and process it fast in order to make decisions that will work in practice.

But there are a few problems with a high IQ, the main one being that we rely on it too much when we are trying to persuade others. We push rational arguments at the people we want to come around to our point of view. Of course people need to believe that ideas will work in practice, that they make sense, and that they are credible. But people also need to feel some affinity with what is being proposed—not just that it makes sense, but also that it feels right. The key verb in the last sentence is *feel*. We want to know that our leaders are believable. As we say in Chapter 2, believability means that a leader is genuine and principled and seen as a trusted and inspirational guide to be followed. There is nothing more persuasive than knowing that someone has our best interests at heart.

We say at the start that strategy is overplanned and underled. Formulating a strategy is intellectual work—selling a strategy so that it gets executed is emotional work. It is insufficient to use logic to get people excited about and emotionally committed to a new strategic direction. We contend that we have concentrated too hard on creating the perfect strategy and in the process we have overemphasized thinking. Leaders at every level, whether they are Elders, the top 100 Village, or others, tend to overplay credibility and underplay believability. Credibility is our Aristotle—we can make rational arguments that hang together. Believability is our Euripides—we behave in authentic and trustworthy ways.

This chapter covers one big idea—thinking can actually get in the way of strategy execution. Not what we think, but how we think and how we overrely on thinking. This idea is at the heart of this book because we believe that leaders need a fundamentally different skill set to execute strategy. Leaders need to move from thinking to feeling in order to stack the odds of successful strategy execution in their favor. Execution is the emotional work of instinct, empathy, and purpose. If we want everyone to own strategy execution, it's precisely the wrong moment to put on our thinking cap. Let's turn first to how we overthink.

Thinking Gets in the Way

The analysts who comment on companies depend on evidence to prove to them that the strategy the company is pursuing is the right one. The organization's credibility is founded on its senior leaders being able to articulate the case. For example, if the goal is global expansion, the market needs to understand why the company intends to move into some geographic regions and not others; why it will start with certain services or products and not others; why it will attack certain customer segments and not others. It's about rational choices and targets and the evidence to back them. Leaders need to support their decisions with at least some data to demonstrate that the strategic choices are well-thought-out, even if they turn out not to be the right ones. We meet these expectations by supplying the statistics and logic that the situation demands. The danger is that leadership communications become too narrowly defined by this process.

We also know that senior executives operate under conditions of extreme uncertainty. Sometimes, the levels of uncertainty are so high that no amount of evidence will be able to point them toward one particular decision. They can pile the data as high as they like, but it's still likely to be pretty evenly balanced between a "go" or a "no-go" decision. They can never know enough. This is where too much thinking can get in the way. It can lead to analysis paralysis, getting stuck in an overthinking loop, continuing to pile up the evidence in the hope that the answer will emerge. Overthinking tends to a bias for collecting and counting the evidence. If it doesn't produce an answer, the data can still be used as a shield to defend against attack, or worse, as a sword to bludgeon forward and demand compliance.

But the world is not linear, ambiguity sits where we would prefer clarity, and black swans do exist.[2] Our schooling and training, wherever in the world we are educated, push us toward making a case backed by facts and figures. We also need to incorporate subjective data and to exercise judgment. Instead of counting the evidence, we need to weigh it. Evidence is only one half of the story. We shouldn't get fixated on evidence at the expense of instinct.

Sweet Irony

The irony is that we make more decisions using instinct than evidence. "The brain doesn't so much calculate, as seethes and waves."[3] That's the first blow to what most of us have historically considered as rational, evidence-based decision making. Our increasing knowledge of how the brain works shows that evidence comes second.[4] Our brain searches for and retrieves evidence and facts to support an idea or a decision that we have already made using our instinct. Experienced executives have finely honed instinct. Jeremy Pelczer, the chairman of WaterAid, believes that "the top line of executives has to trust their instinct in setting priorities and making choices; they become the strategy ambassadors to explain the message to the rest of the workforce."[5] Do you trust your own instinct? Do you use it enough? Exciting research over the last 10 years into how the brain works tells us that you really should.

Trust Your Instinct

Daniel Kahneman was awarded the 2002 Nobel Memorial Prize in Economics for his work, popularized in his book, *Thinking, Fast and Slow*. It is groundbreaking in the diverse insights it offers into how we think and make decisions. A central part of his book is about System 1 and System 2 thinking. System 1 is fast (very fast), while System 2 requires cogitation and concentration. System 1 thinking dislikes ambiguity, so it suppresses doubt and quickly searches for information to confirm its first, instinctive decision. System 2 is slow and ponderous and can result in tunnel vision as we focus in on one topic. Most schoolwork requires effort and therefore needs System 2 thinking to analyze data and to think through ideas and draw conclusions. But in practice, we make many everyday decisions using System 1, our instinct. System 1 constantly feeds impressions, intuitions, intentions, and feelings to System 2, which runs in low-effort mode as much as it can. That is, it will only kick into gear when System 1 gets into trouble and needs more detailed and specific processing to solve a problem.

Emotional Damage

We have traditionally thought about decision making as objective consideration of the facts. How many times have you heard someone at work say something like, "We shouldn't get too emotional over this. We have to think rationally"? In fact, the opposite is true. The second blow to traditional thinking is that decision making is driven by emotion.[6]

There has been a series of studies looking at the impact of damage to two emotional centers of the brain, the ventromedial prefrontal (VMF) cortex and the amygdala. The studies looked at and compared decision-making ability in patients with damage to either of these two centers and compared their abilities with a control group with no damage. In both cases of damage, the patient makes bad decisions when forced to choose and, unlike the control group, doesn't learn to make more advantageous decisions as the exercise proceeds. In real life, as opposed to laboratory conditions, VMF patients appear rational, but enter a continuous and endless System 2 loop over even simple decisions, like which date a meeting should be held on. In one case study, the VMF-damaged individual spent almost half an hour listing the reasons for and against two potential meeting dates, including extraneous considerations such as the possible weather on the day. Perfectly rational but completely indecisive. In this condition, there is no emotional nudge toward what feels like the most advantageous choice, so the individual becomes locked in analysis.

Emotion makes us decide.

In an interesting side note, the VMF is located in the brain just behind the bridge of the nose. In some Asian countries, it is common to paint a colored dot, called a *bindi*, in the center of forehead close to the eyebrows. Traditionally, this area is said to be the sixth chakra, the seat of "concealed wisdom." According to followers of Hinduism, this chakra is the exit point for kundalini energy. The bindi is said to retain energy and strengthen concentration. How did the ancients ever work that out? Modern research giving us the scientific explanation was published only in 1999.

The message here is to understand that we all rely on emotion and instinct. Don't try and isolate decision making from these two influences because they are woven into the fabric of every decision we make.

The Body Shop

Anita Roddick was the founder of The Body Shop in 1976. A rebellious spirit, her world travels after college were curtailed in South Africa where she was ejected for breaking the anti-apartheid laws by attending a jazz club on "nonwhites" night. She returned to her hometown of Littlehampton on the south coast of England, married, had children, and with her husband Gordon, opened first a hotel and then a restaurant. Running both the hotel and restaurant eventually became too demanding on family life. The restaurant was sold, and Roddick's husband declared that he intended to disappear on an ambitious travel expedition—to ride a horse from South America to New York City. Roddick looked for another enterprise on which to concentrate her energy and earn money in her husband's absence. After some thought, she came up with the idea of a cosmetics business with a difference. The difference—natural ingredients.

On March 27, 1976, with her husband about to leave on his travels, Roddick opened for business selling environmentally friendly cosmetics in Brighton, close to Littlehampton. The idea was not just to sell socially responsible products based on natural ingredients, but to sell them in convenient small sample-like sizes tempting customers to try them out. The Brighton store prospered, and soon Roddick was planning another store in nearby Chichester. By the time her husband returned in 1977, The Body Shop concept was unstoppable. Requests to set up branches elsewhere in the country were flooding in. Roddick's friends and family ran the first few shops. To respond to the demand to open shops elsewhere, Roddick and her husband began franchising the concept. A high proportion of franchisees were women, and Roddick could justifiably claim to have helped change the traditional male-dominated image of entrepreneurs in the United Kingdom.

Roddick built her hugely successful business on instinct and principle, not on data and strategic analysis. There was no demand for what she created until her product existed, and then everyone wanted it. What she started was not a conventional cosmetics business. She had little time for the beauty industry, believing that it was in the business of selling unattainable dreams. The Body Shop was different. Roddick made no special claims for her products. In fact she didn't advertise, relying on publicity and then word of mouth to bring customers through the shop doors.

"Making products that work—that aren't part of the cosmetic industry's lies to women—is all important," Roddick has said. "Making sure we minimalize our impact in our manufacturing processes, clean up our waste, put back into the community . . . we go where businesses never want to because they don't think it is the role of business to get involved."[7]

Watch Out for Bias

We are not saying that every executive decision becomes a leap of faith. Executives' strong instinct has been honed by experience. It's been tested out over the years and adjusted when it proved to be right or wrong. You've earned the right to rely on your instinct—it is how you make decisions most of the time. But your instinct, or System 1, will try to convince you that you are always right. So watch out for bias, continue learning to hone your instinct, and keep an open mind. Instinct works best when we are in familiar situations and need to move fast.

Another reason that we underestimate instinct and emotion and place too much weight on so-called rational analysis is that we hire consultants. They sell IQ for a living to help craft strategies and solve organizational problems.

The Consultants Aren't Helping

David Levin, the CEO of UBM, says, "A good strategy is dynamic and markets need both evidence and instinct. The trouble with consultants is that they are all left brain; it is sadly often not creative. Too much data and not enough creativity."[8]

It's rare to walk onto the executive floor in any kind of organization without seeing consultants. They often sit at desks full time alongside the Village Elders. Who are they, and what are they doing? Content consultants have answers to situations that they encounter time and again. Process consultants, on the other hand, help organizations to ask the right questions and challenge traditional thinking. What they all have in common is that they import a tool kit of models, from simple four-box matrices to complex mathematical algorithms. The global consulting industry has compounded overfocus on IQ by proliferating analytical models and charts. Consultants take our problem and turn it into their language. And the special language of strategy gets in the way of execution.

Another CEO explains how this can make life difficult. "The more time you spend trying to fit strategy into boxes, the harder it is to create a message that sells and empowers people to action. Strategy presentations contain magnificent charts and brilliant prose, but you lose the essence of what you are trying to do—it becomes lost in esoteric jargon. Strategy consultants haven't moved on."

They Speak a Different Dialect in Their Village

It's not a lack of comprehension. The CEO understands what the consultants are advising. His challenge is to avoid being hijacked by the jargon so that he can translate strategic direction into simple and direct language that everyone can understand. Business books and consultants have their own language, and it can appear esoteric. Just like the Eskimos, who have lots of words to describe snow,[9] business consultants have lots of words to describe strategy and then lots of models to describe the many different kinds of strategies. The challenge is that this then leaves us trying to create a story that fits into a mold, rather than telling it straight. This CEO goes further: "The danger is that the CEO hears the jargon and chooses to delegate strategy to someone on the team who speaks the same jargon and who can keep up with it. Then the CEO loses ownership or the ability to translate. It's dangerous."

It's almost as if strategy becomes a separate game with its own special rules and language. As a result, even the most senior executive in the business, the CEO, may not feel ownership of the strategy. It's been delegated and turned into models and language that then get lost in translation. If ownership of the strategy is lost at this, the very highest level, the chances of execution are severely diminished. It's like visitors from another village, who speak another language. The consultants come in and facilitate strategy formulation, but then they reshape the strategic conversation into their own dialect. This makes it hard to understand, let alone propagate. Rather than providing clarity, it can become an intellectual puzzle and then become hard to explain in a way that everyone in the company can understand.

More than that, suppose that it's the wrong strategy? Without the business instinct to test it, it's easy for the strategy to go off course. There has to be good, clear dialogue between the consultants and the business leaders, to test that it's the right strategy. But how do we do that, if the language obfuscates the reality? The language sounds clever and convincing. A bit like the emperor with no clothes, maybe we don't like to confess that we don't really understand or that we have significant doubts about what is being proposed.[10] We fit in, and we go along.

Too Powerful?

Consultants can be very powerful. One CEO told a story about his predecessor. Some consultants, hired by the director of research and development, exposed the CEO as apparently being a partial cause of the challenges facing the company. They formed strong alliances with members of the executive team, and, as a result, the CEO lost his job. So their impact can be dramatic. The Elders cannot afford to become so dependent that they allow consultants to make their executive decisions for them. The executives run the risk of the strategy being the consultants' rather than theirs, with a resultant lack of ownership from the top 100 Village. Lack of ownership means no sustainable execution.

Brush Up Your EQ

The development of strategy is the CEO's purpose, but the execution of strategy is a challenge for the whole organization. How can we encourage and lead widespread ownership of strategy execution? We need a new set of skills. We need to make sure that everyone feels an emotional connection with what the organization is trying to achieve.

Nick Forster, former COO of Reed Exhibitions and now personal advisor to their Elders, had a 25-year partnership alongside his CEO, Mike Rusbridge. They were careful to structure the company so that people didn't report to Mike through Nick, who, in his own words, is "in left field of the pyramid." This means that Nick didn't sit in the expected place in the organizational hierarchy, but operated to one side of it, quasi-independently. The advantage this brings is that Forster could indulge his passion for people and for building new business through the old-fashioned virtue of managing by wandering around (MBWA).[11] Because there is no direct reporting relationship to him, people are more relaxed in his company and open in their conversations with him. Forster says, "You need to get out, feel the pulse of the company, relate to what's happening. I know most of the people, and I am there to help them to build their business. I am non-confrontational. I do one-to-one conversations well, and my job is to spend a lot of time thinking and seeing where the opportunities are."[12]

Nick is a real strategist. He spends time talking with people and helping them explore new ideas for the business. He doesn't busy himself with an endless to-do list of his own; he spends a lot of his time thinking. He is absolutely clear that his added value comes through tuning into others and supporting them to expand the businesses. He uses his EQ.

The emotional reality of business has gained a lot of attention over the past 15 years. Through his 1995 book, *Emotional Intelligence,*[13] Daniel Goleman kick-started a wave of reminders that our emotional self is as important as our intellectual self at work. Yet somehow, engaging hearts still doesn't come as naturally as engaging minds. There is an unhelpful balance toward the logical and the rational, which even Mr. Spock[14] found doesn't always work so well in practice.

One senior female executive with over 20 years of experience in the pharmaceutical industry, mostly with AstraZeneca and GlaxoSmithKline who has also held several board positions, is convinced that there is too much rationality in strategy execution. "Rationality is a limiter. Of course you need IQ as well as EQ, but belief in a strategy is emotional; it helps understanding and builds connection to it. High-level debates forget all about emotion, but it energizes us."[15] To get ownership for strategy execution, we need to tune in to how people are feeling about the direction we are asking them to go in.

Why this emphasis on feeling? Because every new strategy brings change, and every change evokes a visceral reaction—always. It can be anything from a small frisson of uncertainty to complete panic, depending on the scale of the change and how closely it affects us. Our reaction may be big or small; it may be positive or negative. But it's emotional.

Just as instinct and emotion play a large part in how we make decisions, so feelings play a large part in how we react to change. And executing a strategy means making change happen.

Predictably Irrational[16]

All human beings go through some predictable stages of emotional reaction in response to change.[17] We are irrational in predictable ways. The first is denial—we are flustered, and we want the world to go back to the way it was before we heard the news. The second stage is anger or emotion of some kind; what is happening feels unfair, or frustrating, or wrong. Then there is a period of bargaining, as we grapple with the reality of the new situation, and try to bring it under our control. Then comes a period of withdrawal as we really process what is happening and try to make sense of it. We experiment with new ways of working and try to figure out ways to move ahead. Finally, we accept the situation—it might continue to make us unhappy, but we learn to live with it and move on. We have woven new practices, beliefs, and routines into our lives. The change process, once complete, provides the basis of our "new normal." Until the next round of change.

These reactions are more of a menu than a recipe. We don't necessarily go through them in exactly this sequence, and sometimes we will loop round more than once. We don't always feel each stage deeply. In contrast, at other times we might get stuck permanently in one stage and fail to move on, unless we can ask for and accept help. Have you ever met anyone like this? Someone who is still feeling angry about some event that happened years ago and has never fully accepted it and so has been unable to integrate it into a new way of being? It's also possible to feel each stage deeply but to keep moving forward, or to move superficially and quickly through the change without intense personal impact. It depends on how big and important the change feels to us.

A Metaphorical Hug

The critical point here is that strategy execution means change, and change is an emotional process. Appealing to logic, citing facts and figures, or careful elucidation of the vision doesn't work. When we're in a state of nervousness or anxiety, we need emotional reassurance or a hug. It's not evidence we seek, but empathy or at least a bit of sympathy. It's a bit like being in an argument at home and your partner looks at you and says, "You don't love me any more." That is not the moment to launch into a list of things you have done that prove your love. It's time to tune into what your partner is feeling and why. It's time for a hug.

This isn't a new management technique. We are not suggesting that you actually go around hugging people at work, although it seemed to work for Herb Kelleher.[18] Rather than literally hugging people at work, try a metaphorical hug. What's a metaphorical hug like? It's listening, it's acknowledging the anxiety, and it's providing space and time for conversations about trepidation and uncertainties. Yet our default tends to be intellectual, to cite again all the good reasons why this route is the right one, to try to move past the uncertainty and the hesitation as fast as possible. Too much thinking with too little empathy simply doesn't work.

It's as if we are afraid that if we stop to ask a question, we won't be able to respond with all the facts at our fingertips, so it's best not to pause. But when they're faced with change, people need to talk and be heard; they don't necessarily need to be answered. It's as if we are in too much of a hurry to get on with it and don't have the time to discuss it. But unless people can make sense of the change in their own way, you can hurry all you like. They won't be hurrying after you.

People Stop Listening, So Stop Talking

The same research on the predictable stages of emotional reaction to change also explains that the more confounded we are by the change we are facing, the less able we are to listen. Fear makes us deaf, and change can be frightening. It's hard enough to listen in normal, everyday life because we think between four and seven times faster than we speak.[19] It's easy for a word or phrase to set our brains racing ahead, thinking about something else. And it's worse when we hear news about a change that is going to affect us. That's when we stop listening to common sense or to careful explanations. In fact, we stop listening completely. Our attention goes inward, as we try to digest the news and work out what it means for us. We need the space and time to reflect. Therefore, if we want people to hear, comprehend, and then move forward with change, we need to be aware of these reactions. If we deal only with the factual impact of change, the what of change and not the emotional reaction it generates, change will have no solid foundation. There is no point in talking when no one is listening.

Recognize It When You See It

Ali Gill is a former Olympic rower. Today she uses her physical prowess in combination with her Oxford psychology degree to help coach and counsel business leaders. One phenomenon she has observed is the anxiety felt by some younger leaders whose rise has been meteoric. "They are promoted fast because they are talented. They then experience a wave of unexpected, and to them inexplicable, feelings. Previously very confident, they find themselves feeling highly anxious and much less certain. I explain to them that it's because they are now leading others who are worried about the changes and uncertain about their futures. Leaders absorb the anxiety that surrounds them; it is often engulfing. This is called 'transference'—the process by which we vicariously experience the feelings of others. These bright young leaders find this hard to get."[20] An important part of emotional intelligence is the ability to connect with and understand your own feelings, to explain what you are feeling and why. This gives you the self-insight to begin to understand what others are feeling.

Let's turn now to think about how we can harness emotional insight to help ourselves and others through change.

A New Skill Set for Execution

How does a new skill set relate to leading strategy execution? We believe that leaders at all levels in the organization need a new set of skills. This means shifting the emphasis away from the IQ it took to build the strategy and toward the EQ that will help others to execute the strategy. Emotion is the missing dimension in creating strategic agility for your organization.[21] Leaders understand intellectually that they need to engage hearts as well as minds, but they often fail to work to get both in practice. We can empathize with another human being only if we understand what emotions that person is feeling. So to engage hearts, we need to press pause on the explanation we are offering about what needs to happen and instead listen to the reactions we are getting and tune in to the level of emotional acceptance. We can persuade others only if we know what they want and can demonstrate to them how it will be delivered. We need to develop our ability to tune in, to have social insight. That's persuasive.

Being Influenced Is Influential

If you want people to join you on the journey, let them influence you. Why do you need to show that you can be influenced? Because we know that it makes you more influential.[22] People who show that they are open to suggestions from others get more of their own ideas accepted in return. As one colleague expresses it, human relationships are about "unarticulated reciprocity."²³ In the vernacular, you scratch my back, and I'll scratch yours. You also need to be open to influence because you might just have it wrong. You are testing that the new strategy is working. Some push-back may be about resistance to change, but at other times it's because execution is off course because the strategy really is the wrong one—for that region or country or product or service. Listen carefully so that you can differentiate between resistance and good advice. Then you can adjust.

Patience Is a Virtue

If you are explaining to someone the strategy and what it will take to execute it, you are already ahead of your audience. You need to be patient while they catch up with you. It can feel frustrating and it can feel slow, but if these negative emotions are apparent to your audience, you will simply compound their natural nervousness in the face of change. In the early stages, you need to be crisp, clear, and calm in your message. This is what's changing, this is what is staying the same, and this is how we need to respond. And you need to say it more than once to get the message across—because people are bound up in their internal thought processes as they digest the news and try to work out what it means for their future. As leaders of change we need to be patient. Expect to have to repeat a consistent message many times and also expect to spend time going through how the change will have a specific impact on the individuals concerned.

Control Your Own Emotions

Don't overreact to push-back in the early stages. We want to feel some resistance, because otherwise it means that the message isn't getting through. We need to hold onto our own emotional reactions while we let others vent theirs. Empathy isn't the same as agreeing with dissenters. We are simply acknowledging their point of view as we work to move them toward the personal changes that they will need to make.

We can offer support and advice, but no let-out clauses. The consistent message must be calm: "This is going to happen. How can I help you?" It's really important not to suppress arguments and conflict at this stage—we want the emotions expressed and out in the open. Of course, we should expect people to remain as professional as possible at all times. But conflict and debate are signs that the message has penetrated and that the process of adjustment has started. Take it as a positive sign. Too often we take this questioning phase as a sign of rebellion and clamp down hard, piling on the arguments for the change and tightening the measures. This pushes people away from us, into denial and apathy, rather than pulling them toward us with curiosity and interest.

Connect, Connect, Connect

Every book on strategy talks about "communicate, communicate, communicate." And each one of them is wrong. What springs to mind when we say, "You need to communicate this message"? Most of us start to think about preparing a presentation or writing an e-mail or at the very least getting our story straight in our head. We are getting something ready to deliver. And now, what comes to mind when we say "connect"? Somehow the next word that springs to mind is "with." There is a connotation of togetherness. The tendency for communication to be associated with transmitting a message is only exacerbated by tweeting and blogging, where messaging is not reliant on anyone responding. Instead, think "connect."

Set time aside for conversations. Your calendar gets full of activities and events, meetings, and conferences. You are kept very busy. But how well-leveraged are you? That is, how many followers do you have who really understand what needs to be done to make the strategy happen, who truly believe in it as much as you do, and who can act in unison, without guidance? They are like an extension of you. How many colleagues across the business can you truly claim believe the same things you do—that is, all working together to execute the strategy, not inadvertently working at cross purposes or undermining each other? If you can clear space in your calendar to talk to people, to influence, persuade, and, even more importantly, be influenced, then you are moving toward alignment. Execution will start to happen.

Good quality conversation is critical to effective strategy execution. Yet time and again, we fail to make space for this in our calendars. We focus too much on doing our own job and completing our own tasks at the expense of taking time to spread our influence.

One CEO told us: "I spent hours and hours just walking the plant and the office corridors. Hundreds and hundreds of conversations, tuning in to where people were in our journey and talking about the future I could see. Giving them a sense of what we were creating together. Four years later we were there, our vision had become reality. My most important task was to socialize the ideas to help us to get where we wanted to be."

Effective communication is the absolute opposite of telling others what to do via a PowerPoint presentation. Just as this CEO advises, it's good quality conversation with key players who can take your influence and spread it farther.

Be the Change You Want to See[24]

People are great boss watchers. (They even talk about you when they get home.) Your words and actions are continually observed, dissected, and interpreted. They are checked for match, to see if you do what you say, and for sense. They will mimic what you do rather than what you say, because you communicate much louder through your actions than through your words. So if you tell people that customers are important, make sure you spend time with customers. If you want people to focus on expanding into a new region, spend visible time there. If you want it to be OK to talk about how change feels, talk about how it makes you feel. You have more impact than you imagine or realize. One CEO wanted the company to present a "smarter" image to customers, so he started wearing a necktie. Within weeks, 80 percent of male employees were also wearing neckties, without any company edict being sent out about a new dress code. We watch leaders for clues all the time.

And remember, if you find yourself bemoaning that "they just don't get it," pause to consider if they don't get it because it looks like you don't get it. We may talk collaboration, but what if they see us openly fighting with colleagues? We may talk going global, but what if the senior leaders all come from the country where headquarters is located? If we don't practice what we preach, neither will they. Spending time doing whatever it is that you are telling employees is important to get the strategy executed. Actions always speak louder than words. We need to be tuned in to feelings and expectations and live the messages we are transmitting.

It's Physical

In the rush of doing the job, we can neglect how we come across. Leading execution is a physical as well as an intellectual and emotional process. People watch not just what we say, but also how we say it and how we look. Are we happy, concerned, worried, joyful, or anxious? It needs to show on the outside. If we know that, in repose, we naturally look worried, we need to make a conscious effort to smile. If it's hard to distinguish our thoughtful expression from our blank expression, we should practice making some sage faces in the mirror. This is not a trivial exercise, as Dr Albert Mehabrian's research shows.[25] A large percentage of meaning is communicated nonverbally, and dissonance between what is being said and how it is being said makes people on the receiving end of the mixed message uncomfortable. Observers are looking for a congruent picture. If you say that the strategy is going well, look like you mean it. Or if you are dissatisfied with the rate of progress toward your execution targets, don't walk around smiling. Align what you want to express with what you show on the outside.

Close the gap between what you intend to say and what you actually communicate. Spend as much time thinking about your nonverbal behavior as you do about the content of what you are going to communicate. "Use a picture. It's worth a thousand words," appeared in a 1911 newspaper article quoting newspaper editor Arthur Brisbane discussing journalism and publicity.[26] He was right. The first impression people will have about your message is how you look, before you even open your mouth. So plan your appearance. Spend time planning how to express your ideas and your tone of voice and demeanour, as well as planning the content of what you intend to say. Nonverbal communication is a powerful tool, but it can also work against us if we are sending mixed messages.

Give Them Confidence

Albert Bandura is the David Starr Jordan professor emeritus of social science in psychology at Stanford University. He is known as the originator of social learning theory and the theory of self-efficacy. A 2002 survey ranked Bandura as the fourth most frequently cited psychologist of all time (behind B. F. Skinner, Sigmund Freud, and Jean Piaget) and as the most-cited living one.

Imagine the scene on the opening day of Stanford's Executive Program. The classroom is full of senior executives and serving CEOs. The class is divided into two halves, and the white-coated Bandura instructs each half separately on the identical exercise that it is about to undertake. His white coat gives him extra authority. One half of the class is told how challenging it will find the exercise, but that intelligence is not fixed, so members of that half will learn a lot and develop themselves during the afternoon, as well as have fun. The second half of the class is told how challenging it will find the exercise and that because intelligence is fixed, members of this half will struggle and become frustrated, but they need to push through and achieve as much as they can.

At the end of the afternoon the two halves of the class are brought together to talk about the exercise. The half that was told it would learn and have fun did just that—the mood is high and the results are good. The other half of the class hasn't done nearly as well and is frustrated and bad-tempered. Members of this half demand to do the same exercise that the other half of the class has enjoyed so much (recall that the exercise was the same for both halves). Same exercise, different outcomes.

What happened? People rise to your expectations of them. If you tell them that strategy execution will be challenging but that it will also give them the opportunity to develop and have fun, that's what will happen. And if you tell them that it will be hard work and frustrating, then they'll end up downcast and frustrated. As a leader, you have at least the same amount of influence as a white-coated scientist at Stanford University. How will you tell your employees to be?

Keep Up with Them

One final thought: As the pulse of the execution process, you are shepherding people, cajoling, persuading, engaging, and connecting. At some point you will see success and realize that they have moved on. Have you been so busy getting them to move that you have forgotten to move yourself? Don't let them get ahead of you. Plan the next moves at the same time as you encourage execution of the current strategy.

Connecting with Purpose

So where are we in the narrative? Emotional intelligence is a critical capability for someone leading strategy execution, and it is regularly underexercised at work. Most leaders default to evidence and logic when they make the case for change. If the audience is a market analyst, they need the rationale and the logic. If the audience is someone who needs to buy into the change to make the new strategy happen, they need to feel safe and confident about the future. The distinction is that the analyst will use commentary to advise people about the company as an investment opportunity. It's a very different proposition internally. You are changing the life of the employee whom you want to persuade to behave or think in different ways.

When we want to persuade and influence someone inside the business, it's a mistake to focus on facts and data to sell change. To move people inside the business, we need to tune into where they are in the emotional change journey, listen, and offer support. Pull them toward us through understanding their needs, rather than drive them ahead of us with our logic. It's much easier to urge people on to execute the strategy if it honestly feels more important to them than just another day's work for another day's pay. Working life has to be about more than the next set of quarterly results or the next paycheck. What is the purpose of all this activity?

We say at the start that successful strategy execution requires a different skill set for leaders. Execution is about instinct, empathy, and purpose. Let's move onto the third topic and look at the importance of purpose in strategy execution.

Purpose and Passion

Ginni Rometty is chairperson, president, and chief executive officer of IBM. She was appointed on October 1, 2012 amid great fanfare as one of the then 4 percent of female Fortune 500 CEOs and the first female CEO in IBM's 101-year history. Within nine months of her tenure, the stock price reached its highest-ever level. Two days after she took the job, she was interviewed by Jessi Hempel at *Fortune's* Most Powerful Women Summit. A CEO's most important job is thinking long term and reinventing the company as the world changes. Rometty told the audience, after being introduced by Time Inc. editor in chief, John Huey, that she thinks the key aspect in accomplishing this important job is not the strategy, but "strategic belief."[27] When asked about her strategy, she responded: "Ask me what I believe first, that's a way more enduring answer." What does she mean? In a world where everything is changing so quickly, we cannot predict the future, so our strategy, or plan, can go awry. A plan can be well-thought-out, intensely researched, and minutely detailed—and it can also be wrong. In an increasingly volatile world, a plan isn't enough. Rometty is making the case for a broader and less specific sense of direction—destiny rather than target.

Rometty continued: "Most of us have workforces that are very bright, very intelligent, that want to be engaged in a broad way. This idea of strategic belief is saying that you can agree amongst the firm for the future, on some really big arcs of change." The example she gives for IBM is her belief that the era of cognitive computing, where computers start to learn, rather than just being programmed, is starting now and will completely change IBM. It's essential that IBM follow this long-term, "directional arc."

What Rometty is doing is giving people a sense of direction and purpose. She is responding to a basic human drive.[28] She is also demonstrating very clearly her belief and conviction about the future she is describing, which is powerful because our colleagues want to see that we're emotionally committed.[29]

We've already talked about the typical strategy briefing. The long PowerPoint presentation, charts, colors, targets, and gap analysis—we are here and we need to get to there. Here's how far we have to go to make it happen. Here are the obstacles that could stop us. The briefing will be long on information but won't grab the heart. Rometty is working at a different level. She is engaging at the level of belief, our conviction about the future. Now that really does get us engaged. We can become passionate about our beliefs. And no one can tell us we are wrong because belief, like emotion, is ours to feel and own. Our debate about beliefs will involve passion and conviction, and those are the first steps on the road toward ownership of the outcome. Not dispassionate debate about the facts, which are outside us and can be treated objectively. Instead it's a debate that touches us and our values more deeply—passionate engagement about the right thing to do.

What Does It Take to Change Your Mind?

Strategy execution generally means hundreds and thousands of people agreeing on a new direction and adopting a new set of beliefs and behaviors. In these days of complexity and uncertainty, with constant innovation attacking our current business models and ways of work, strategy means doing something different, rather than doing more of the same.

There is ongoing debate about the right way to change someone's mind. It's an important topic for strategy execution, because a new strategy brings change and change demands a different outlook and new ways of working. The debate is generally about the route to follow: whether to change someone's mind and wait for the expected new behaviors to follow or whether to change their behavior, which will lead them to a new set of beliefs. In line with our overrational approach to strategy execution, many writers favor the "change their behavior" route because it is generally considered to be faster than working on someone's outlook or mindset. In model after model,[30] what is going on inside someone's head falls far down on the list of things to address in order to execute strategy. The rationale is that you can change people's behavior by measuring and rewarding them for the new behaviors that you want to see, that is, by changing the performance measurement system. And it works, up to a point. Up to the point where we know that not every performance management system rewards the right behaviors (as opposed to getting business results). And not every performance management system is used properly (it can end up as an annual exercise in checking off boxes, rather than being used for day-to-day management).

Ideally what we want is for everyone to believe in the new strategy and to own its execution. The advantage of ownership is that, as a leader, you are not constantly watching people to ensure that they are complying with strategy execution. Compliance is at the wrong end of the scale because it means that people will only do what is being asked while you watch them. As soon as you stop watching them, they will regress. It's time consuming and frustrating. At the other end of the scale lies commitment. Commitment means that people have fully bought in to what needs to happen. They don't need to be watched, they can be trusted to do what must be done. They progress with execution unsupervised. And once you can change the way that someone thinks, their behavior will change to match. If they feel commitment and ownership, they will be off and running without the need for constant checking. How hard is it to change mindset instead of starting with changing behavior first?

Helping People to Believe in the Right Things

The good news is that there is a simple and powerful psychological tool at leaders' disposal, and Rometty is onto it. The technical term for it is "cognitive dissonance,"[31] which is a fancy way of saying that our simple human brains like to believe in one thing at a time. For example, if you like generous people and a friend is super careful with money, you have two choices: to rid yourself of the friend or to convince yourself that the friend is not really parsimonious at all. What you cannot do is live with a belief in generosity and a stingy friend. Cognitive dissonance kicks in, and your brain needs to decide on which side of the fence it sits. A classic illustration of cognitive dissonance gives us the modern phrase "sour grapes." In the fable *The Fox and the Grapes* by Aesop (around 580 B.C.), a fox sees some high-hanging grapes and wants to eat them but can't reach them. So the fox decides that the grapes are probably not worth eating and are not ripe or may even be sour. This example follows the pattern: you want something, find it unattainable, so you reduce your dissonance by dismissing or criticizing it. If you can't reduce or eliminate dissonance, you will be in disequilibrium and experience a whole host of emotional reactions, such as frustration, dread, guilt, or anxiety. We are all motivated to reduce dissonance and remove the distress of having an opinion that doesn't fit with others.

How does this help you, as a leader, to execute strategy? Like Rometty, you need to hold up a compelling belief or purpose that people can buy into. If people believe in the overall purpose and you can show them how their current practices and behaviors don't fit, they will be happy to change their behavior to rid themselves of dissonance. The belief or purpose is not a target or a goal or a set of metrics. It is visionary and directional and broad enough for many to buy into. Make it desirable and attainable (unlike the grapes). It evokes desire, and it motivates action.

More Than Charisma

To embed the change, of course, you then need to follow through and ensure that systems (like the reward system) and structures (like individual decision-making scope) fit with the purpose. We pick up these aspects again in more detail in Chapter 5. You also need to ensure that people have the personal capability to execute (training), and they need to see you acting in a way that supports the purpose too.[32] But instead of making systems and behavioral compliance your default starting position, you are making these the second and third steps in strategy execution. If you like, you are starting your change journey at the top end of Maslow's hierarchy of needs,[33] with our human instinct for personal growth and self-actualization, rather than at the bottom end, the territory of survival and compliance.

This is not an argument for charismatic leadership. As engaging as charismatic leaders are, if they overrely on the power of their personality to get things done, then they leave a gaping hole when they move on. The follow-through, to embed change through systems and structures, may never happen. This is, however, an argument for offering people purpose and meaning, rather than facts and figures, to engage their discretionary effort in the work of strategy execution.

Make It Mean Something

Have you heard the apocryphal story about building a cathedral? It is attributed to a variety of people, (even Wikipedia fails to identify its source) including Sir Christopher Wren when he was overseeing the construction of St. Paul's Cathedral in London, completed in 1710. Three stonecutters, busy cutting stone, are each asked what they are doing. One replies, "I am cutting a stone," and the second says, "I am cutting this block of stone to make sure that it is square, and its dimensions are uniform, so that it will fit exactly in its place in a wall." The third stonecutter, who is visibly the happiest worker, replies, "I am building a cathedral." The third stonecutter sees a direct relationship between the work he is doing and the greater vision he is helping to achieve and is therefore more motivated and engaged by his work.

This link between meaning (why I am doing this work) and the work itself (what I am doing) dates back to 1976, when researchers identified three critical aspects that imbue work with meaning.[34] These are skill variety (how many different aspects of the work I must master), task identity (how closely I identify with the task), and task significance (how important is the task). The first two stonecutters have the first two in place—variety and love of the task. But it is only the third stonecutter who adds the third element, sees the bigger picture, and understands how important his task is to building the cathedral. Therefore, he is the most motivated of the three. So, as a leader, your first step in creating meaning for others is to help them to see the link between what they are doing and its contribution to the overall vision for your organization.

Newer research, by Teresa Amabile and Steven Kramer, adds a further slant on sustaining meaning at work.[35] In their book, they describe a multiyear study and conclude that of all the events that can engage people most deeply in their jobs, the single most important is a sense of making progress in meaningful work. Amabile and Kramer explain that progress can be as small as incremental steps forward (small wins). In the same way that we have known for a while the power of MBWA, managing by wandering around, we have also understood the importance of celebrating small wins. Small wins boost what they call "inner work life." Inner work life, or the individual's emotions, motivations, and perceptions related to the work has an impact on creativity, productivity, commitment, and collegiality, and all these have a direct impact on the bottom line.

You now have a straightforward recipe. If you can ensure that people you lead can see how the work they do makes an important contribution and if they get a sense of consistent progress, they will be more motivated, and your overall results will improve.

Just Big Kids, Really

Isn't the reality that you already knew this? As a parent, aunt, uncle, guardian, or grandparent, isn't this how we raise children to achieve and prosper? We explain to them how studying for the dreaded math exam will help them get into college or get a job (keeping their eye on the bigger picture), and we reward their progress with gold stars or other small, simple acknowledgments of achievement. We grow up, in that we age and mature, but our basic human psychology remains the same. We are still motivated by feedback that demonstrates our progress, and we want to understand why the task that we are engaged in is important. The problem is that, as we grow up, we mistake being more adult with being more factual and evidence-based and serious. It doesn't seem "grown up" to expect the small acknowledgments of achievement we received as children. Surely we are beyond that now. Isn't it childish to need feedback or reinforcement? Shouldn't we be more mature, more-self-contained, more self-sufficient?

Well, actually, no.

As a leader, your impact is disproportional, so it's easy for you to create or destroy meaning for people at work. To create meaning, it's important to value others' ideas, to help people feel a sense of achievement and completion, and to help them link what they do on a daily basis to what the organization will achieve over many years. As Amabile and Kramer say, "A sense of purpose in the work, and consistent action to reinforce it, has to come from the top."[36]

Put Meaning First

Simon Sinek's TED Talk has had over 10 million hits. It is called "How Great Leaders Inspire Action." In a stunningly simple idea, he explains that exceptional leaders, from Steve Jobs at Apple to Martin Luther King, stand out because of the way they communicate. In the trilogy "what, how, why," the ordinary leader tells the story in that order. Great leaders, however, start with "why" and only then explain "how" and "what." In essence, great leaders start with the cause, the purpose, the belief. They put meaning first.

The challenge is that the tug of the rational, analytical world works the other way. We tend to start with the overall task (for example, a 20 percent increase in penetration in the emerging economies). Then we work out how to achieve this, through setting milestone targets and deliverables and identifying and overcoming obstacles. Next we try to ensure that the organization is hard-wired for success by aligning structures and systems to reinforce efficient task completion. We go straight to the head. Purpose and meaning are often completely left out of the loop, or perhaps choreographed into the CEO's planned and tightly orchestrated presentation at the annual strategy conference.

Think Differently

Thinking differently is how to create purpose and meaning at work. If we want people to own strategy execution, rather than simply comply with it, we need to change the way they think about it. We start with purpose—why the activity is important, not what the activity is. They need to see strategy execution as powerful work that they own. The next is to create meaning, which is a personal connection to the overall purpose. To feel meaning, they need to see the set of tasks they undertake as significant and linked to a higher purpose. And last, as they move forward, we need to celebrate small wins and victories so that progress is tangible.

To execute the strategy, trust your instinct and start with purpose to appeal directly to the hearts of those you need to follow you.

Summary

In this chapter we take a long, hard look at the new skill set that leaders need in order to incite everyone to execute strategy. We conclude that most strategies are overplanned and underled. Leaders are smart, whether they are Elders, the top 100 Village, or anywhere else in the organization, and that's a positive. The conundrum we face is that to implement a strategy means importing change into the organization, and the human response to change is emotional, not intellectual or rational. Your intellectual strength can become a weakness if that's all you employ to persuade people to change. It's a waste of heart.

Instead of relying too much on rational analysis and logic, make sure that your emotional intelligence is as well-developed and deployed as your IQ. Specifically, work to understand the emotional reactions we all go through when we are faced with change and then deal appropriately with each stage in the change process by developing social insight and empathy. This isn't about being "soft." It's about being effective. An ounce of belief is worth more than a ton of impenetrable PowerPoint presentations. Helping people to navigate change is emotional work. Leaders need to be influential and persuasive, patient, calm, and in control of their own emotions. Where most strategy books recommend "communicate, communicate, communicate," we recommend "connect, connect, connect." It's not about transmitting, it's about engaging. Above all, show how confident you are in their success, because they will perform better if you can do this.

If you want people as to be as committed to change as you are, talk about the greater purpose that the organization is pursuing. Help them to make the connections between this purpose and what they do every day at work in order to add true meaning to their daily routine. If they can see this link, they will be committed to changing, and you will know that you can trust them to do the right things. Strategy execution won't just start, it will stick.

With your strategy execution tool kit for change in place, let's now turn to Chapter 4 to discuss how you can use these skills to instill a culture for execution.

4

Energize People

Leadership is hard to define and good leadership even harder. But if you can get people to follow you to the ends of the earth, you are a great leader.
—Indra Nooyi

The Swanborough Tump

Liz Mellon's maiden name is Swanborough. Although the name has an aristocratic ring, it is in fact pure peasant, dating back to before AD 800. In AD 871, King Alfred and his brother Ethelred met at the Swanborough Tump to source an assembly of fighting men to respond to the Danes who were attacking Wessex from their base at Reading. The Tump is the meeting (or moot) place of the Swanborough Hundred, a hillock (actually a Bronze Age barrow) in the county of Wiltshire and mentioned in the will of King Alfred. The name *Swana beorh* appears in a charter of 987 and is thought to mean "barrow of the peasants."

A hundred is a geographic division formerly used in England, Wales, South Australia, and some parts of Europe, and the United States. It divides a larger region into smaller administrative divisions. In England and Wales, a hundred was the division of a shire for administrative, military, and judicial purposes under common law. Hundreds were widely used as the only intermediary between the parish and the county until the introduction of districts by the Local Government Act 1894. Originally, when introduced by the Saxons between 613 and 1017, a hundred had enough land to sustain approximately 100 households, defined as the land covered by 100 "hides" and was headed by a *hundred-man* or *hundred eolder*. No place in the district of Swanborough has ever grown bigger than a village and today includes several such as Wilcot, Manningford Abbots, and Stanton St. Bernard.

What is the point of this esoteric story? The Tump was the meeting place for 100 units, varying in size from a household to a village, up to 24 times a year. At meetings, taxes were assessed and paid, fighting men gathered for war, disputes were settled, and a variety of legally binding decisions were reached. These regular, face-to-face meetings were used to run every aspect of the district.

In a similar way, today's businesses or organizations are a collection of units, or villages. It's not just about the senior Village (the top 100) and how they communicate with the rest. It's about how a whole collection of villages (business units, functions, geographies, and different management levels) keep communicating and working together to make decisions and set priorities. Our modern challenge is to do this on a larger scale and across a much more widespread geography.

The Tump in Action

There is a great management exercise about strategy execution. Imagine the scene. A room with about 35 executives, divided into three unequally sized groups. The largest group leaves the room first and is taken to a new location with a mysterious grid laid out on the floor. The members of this group represent the workers, but they have no guidelines on what to do next. The second group departs for a separate location, bland and anonymous, with the briefest of instructions on acting as the middle managers, liaising between the workers and the third group, the senior executives. The members of the third and smallest group are taken to a small room, remote from the other two groups. Their surroundings are comfortable, luxurious almost, with a fruit basket, coffee, and cakes. They have a full set of instructions for the task to be achieved over the next 45 minutes. They are the only ones who know what to do. They have been randomly chosen as the leaders, and they have to decide quickly how to lead their tiny organization of 35 people to successfully execute the strategy they have in front of them. Each group is given the means to communicate with the others.

Eighty percent of the time, the exercise concludes with the objective unmet. The task, explained in full to the smallest and most senior group, never gets completed. In essence, strategy execution fails. Why? Each group has its own particular role to play, leading either toward success or failure. Often the most senior group fails to communicate clearly enough, or fast enough, with the other two groups, and its messages are too garbled and piecemeal to make sense. Or sometimes members of this group try to run the exercise in a tightly (too tightly) controlled way from their room. At other times they lack a sense of urgency, and so the task is executed too ponderously to meet the deadline.

It's not always the senior executives who lead the exercise to fail. Sometimes the second group of middle managers compounds or confounds the efforts of the senior group. These middle managers may act like a mailbox, running between the two groups with messages that fail to add context or meaning—lacking perceived value, their exhortations are ignored. At other times they fail to be clear enough with the senior group about the information and clarity they need in order to move into action. Often they are not coordinated and cannot agree among themselves on what needs to be done. And even if the senior and middle managers act quickly and are in accord, the exercise can still fail. Sometimes the third and largest group of workers fails to act in the right way. This group is always keen to get on and do something. In the absence of instructions, its members create activities that keep them busy, but which they suspect are meaningless. By the time they do receive clear instructions, it's too late to divert the workers from whatever activity they have engaged in to keep productive while the more senior teams prevaricated and debated. Or sometimes, when the instructions arrive, they over- and reinterpret them, sacrificing action for debate. At other times, they are too risk-averse to move with the speed and conviction required to meet the deadline.

IQ Doesn't Help

Whatever the reason and at whichever organizational level the fault lies, the collective IQ of approximately 4,375 points is absolutely no help at all in getting the simple task completed.[1] At its worst, the room erupts in recriminations and finger-pointing about who was at fault. At best, the executives all look into the mirror that the exercise holds up to them, and they find themselves wanting. Too indecisive, too slow, unclear, and risk-averse. And if we can't be successful in a group of just 35 people, it teaches us a lot about the real challenges facing us in strategy execution in a global company with thousands of employees spread across many countries.

The exercise is about communication, ownership, and follow-through. It's the same in real business, when we are trying to make strategy happen. And the failure rate is high. In a study of 125,000 employees representing more than 1,000 companies, government agencies, and not-for-profits in over 50 countries, in three out of every five organizations, employees rated their organization weak at execution.[2] When asked if they agreed with the statement, "Important strategic and operational decisions are quickly translated into action," the majority answered no.

We Can Do Better

It's always about communication. It's a question of math. Strategy formulation and development is in the hands of a small number of senior executives—largely, the Elders. But execution means that those simple constructs must be communicated, interpreted, reinterpreted, reframed, and repositioned into the daily reality of thousands of employees. Most just want to turn up, do a decent job, and feel properly valued for their contribution. They may not understand, or even care about, the difficulties and challenges senior executives face in deciding on their four to five strategic priorities. They just want to get on with whatever it is they think they are being asked to do. The trouble is that what seems obvious to the CEO and executive team is far from obvious to the masses deep inside the organization. Unless it is explained simply and clearly, in teams and across networks from the Village of 100 downward, they will find ways of making the strategic messages fit their world. In the absence of direction, they won't just sit and wait, and, with the best of intentions, they may well set off in the wrong direction. So it's a communications game and more—it's about connecting through two-way communications.

It's also definitely about ownership. In strategy execution, those closest to the top of the organizational pyramid work most comfortably with broad frameworks and loose definitions of what is required. They like to have the flexibility to adjust and adapt if results are different from those they anticipated. They take a holistic view and are comfortable dancing with ambiguity. Farther out from this helicopter view, the definitions get tighter and tighter in order to ensure complete adherence to the call for change. There is much less room for anyone to maneuver or deviate from the prescribed approach and process. But this is a mistake. Just as when the management exercise fails, it's because the top executives try to manage execution through control and explicit instruction. People have no room to maneuver and so start to feel like disenfranchised cogs in a wheel. They can't see how their actions contribute to organizational purpose and the greater good, and they grow disheartened and disinterested.

It should be the opposite way around.

The Elders need to discipline themselves to agree on four to five key deliverables and to hold themselves tightly accountable for these, while giving freedom to those trying to execute the strategy to improvise on it as necessary. So to reverse this, it's about ownership of the right thing to do, at the right level. It's about empowerment and accountability.

But at its most fundamental, it's about follow-through. The time-scales for strategy and execution have been swapped over the last decade. Strategy used to be about the long-term view, feeding into a well-documented 5- to 10-year journey. Execution was what took you from milestone to successful milestone every year in between. But a combination of business scandals like the one at Enron, the global financial crash in 2008, the ongoing shift of power, and trade from west to east and from north to south, and the ever voracious Internet have shrunk strategy timescales beyond recognition. There is so much noise in the system that executives have lost confidence in their ability to attack the long term with vigor. One of Peter Drucker's famous quotes is, "The best way to predict your future is to create it."[3] The turbulence of the modern world seems to have eviscerated the appetite for creating the future and has lowered the executive horizon to simply surviving the future.

Connecting for a Culture of Execution

Jeremy Pelczer, the chairman of WaterAid and ex-CEO of Thames Water, is unequivocal. "One of the phrases I have learned that has had a big impact on me is that culture eats strategy for breakfast." So we'd better get the culture right, or, however brilliant our strategy is, we are going nowhere.[4]

We hear a lot about developing a culture for execution without being clear about what that really means. Communication, ownership, and follow-through. That's the recipe for a culture of execution. We are trying to create a culture in the organization that supports and embeds execution rather than unwittingly fighting against it. Let's take each of the components in turn, starting with communication—our human need to connect.

It's a Communications Game

One of the most striking things about John Chambers, CEO of Cisco, is his ability to communicate, to really connect with others. He gets the importance of communication, and he practices it all the time. His leadership is visible and vocal. He will talk until he's hoarse. A really memorable piece of footage is of him hosting a birthday breakfast at Cisco (if it's your birthday that month, you can attend) and taking a challenging question about change. The questioner, a woman, asks whether more change is really needed. Chambers' reply is a master class in itself. If you were asked that question, what would you say? Would you have your answer ready, with three or four good reasons why change never stops? If so, you'd be communicating one-way, not really connecting.

Chambers is disarming. He doesn't try to push his reality onto the woman, who has been working hard and is clearly weary. His reply is a question. "Who, here, thinks we still need to change?" A forest of hands shoots into the air in agreement. People are intelligent and worldly; they don't need him to explain to them why change never stops, and his reply pays them the compliment of understanding how smart and realistic they are. It also cleverly avoids a potentially long debate of the "yes, it is; no, it isn't" variety. This is a master class in communicating and shows the powerful impact of a simple question.

Ban the Cascade

Communication is categorically not one-way and not always from the top down. We think the term "cascade briefing" should be banned. It implies that information has to flow from the top downwards. In reality, fast, honest, and open communication needs to flow freely in every direction.

Let's revisit the management exercise we started out with. When the senior executives are first given their complete instructions on how the game should be played, they disappear into their own world as they try to work out what they should be doing. They want to be really clear on the task before they communicate anything (after all, they are senior executives and have a reputation to uphold). They result is that they talk to each other for too long and neglect their employees. The impact of this lack of communication makes the middle managers look and feel foolish. They run between the senior executives and the workers with nothing to say, but with a desire to act, as they are instructed, as a conduit between the two groups. This is activity without context and therefore without meaning. The workers, meanwhile, fill the void by deciding for themselves what needs to be done. Every time the middle managers come into the room, they ask for instruction: "What is our objective? What is our task? What are we supposed to do?" And every time they fail to get a clear answer, they lose faith in the middle managers' ability to add value and so discount their opinion and continue to do so throughout the rest of the exercise. Once some instructions start to filter through, the action tends to move to the worker level, as the workers strive to complete the task under time pressure. There is a sense of crisis because so little time is left, but once the task is clear, they immediately make suggestions on how to improve the efficiency of execution. They want to do a good job. Now it's the senior executives who feel isolated and out of the communication loop. Desperate for feedback, they sit lonely and uncertain as they wait for reassurance of progress toward the strategic goals they have set. The senior executives feel out of control when they don't hear back. Effective communication is a constant flow, back and forth, up and down, from side to side.

Keep Talking

It's striking how close a simple 45-minute exercise can get to real life at work. Each of the three groups falls out of the communication loop at some point in the exercise, with bad results in each case. When it happens to the senior executives, they lose touch with how their strategy is being executed and feel nervous and out of control. When it happens to the middle managers, they can add no value and so feel humiliated and foolish. When it happens to the workers, they engage in activity, but they know it is probably meaningless, so they become truculent and disaffected. How do we create today's version of the Tump, where information can be publicly shared between the different villages and where disparate interests can be quickly resolved?

It reminds us strongly that communication is a two-way flow. It's not enough for senior executives to instigate a cascade of information—fast—from top to bottom in the organization. It's vital to get the feedback loop going back up to the top too.[5] Has everyone really understood what needs to happen? Are people playing their right roles? What evidence do we have that the strategy is working? We can answer these questions only if we talk to each other up, down, and across the organization. Effective communication is dialogue, not monologue.

It can become a negative or a positive spiral, and each management level has a different and specific role to play in making it work. Obviously, most organizations have more than three layers, but let's keep it simple here by thinking about only three: connecting the top, middle, and those closest to the action at the bottom.

Connecting from the Top

The CEO and the executive team were meeting periodically over two days with a selection of executives from the Village (the top 100). The objective was for the executives to understand the new strategy about to be launched by the company. It was partly a process of education and partly a process of motivation and retention (the executives would feel special, with privileged access to inside information). As they huddled in small groups in a variety of changing configurations, questions and observations from the executives flew thick and fast. Each observation was painstakingly explained and each question was answered by the Elders.

To an outside observer, the dynamic was obvious. The members of the executive team thought they were being asked questions of clarification and so responded with greater detail and depth. It was striking that none of them wrote down anything the executives were saying, but they just kept expanding on the themes. The Villagers were actually trying, politely and supportively, to point out glaring gaps in how the strategy would actually work in practice in the different geographies served by the company. There were some problematic assumptions being made by headquarters that would lead to disconnects in the market. In short, there were aspects of this strategy that simply weren't going to work in practice.

The executive team saw it as their role to communicate, that is, to expound and explain. They had forgotten that real communication is an exchange, a true connection.

Despite the complex and ambiguous world we live in today, with data freely available to all and a widespread ability to use experience to turn these data into useful and meaningful information, an inherent assumption persists that the more senior executives know best. It simply isn't so. It's not their job to explain to the rest of the organization what needs to happen. The executive team needs to see itself as just one of the villages meeting at the Tump. Its members have information available to them that others don't have, but they need to recognize that the other villages are in exactly the same place. It's about understanding that each village at the meeting has a role of equal value to play in order for the strategy to be executed—different roles, but of equal value.

Speak the Local Dialect

Of course, the most senior villagers have to make the final decision, but it will be a good decision only if they take into account the realities that only the other villages can see. The top 100 Village has its own dialect, as do all the villages (finance, sales, marketing, and so on all have their own special languages). The trick is to be multilingual. And it's not just about speaking the right language. It's also about saying something often enough so that everyone moves beyond hearing, to real understanding. All too often the Elders and the Villagers think that they have said it loudly and clearly enough, when they really haven't.

Not Everyone Is a Natural

Not everyone is a natural communicator. Irene Dorner, president and CEO of HSBC America, knows that communicating the strategy is vital, so she wasn't going to let any of her Elders off the hook. She has the social insight to know them well enough to help: "I spoke to two senior people who I knew would struggle to communicate clearly; one got a coach, the other undertook to introduce the strategy and then delegate the presentation to someone more able."[6] Even where a senior executive like these men lacks the capacity to develop good communication skills, he still has to own the communication for the strategy, even if he doesn't do the communicating himself. The alternative is untenable—to work around him. However committed he is to the strategy, the rumors would have started that his silence translated to dissent. If people start to believe that the Elders aren't wholeheartedly committed to the strategy, then their own execution of it becomes optional.

Be Memorable

We know that stories are up to 22 times more memorable than facts and figures alone.[7] We tell our children stories to teach them lessons about life that they can easily remember, and stories serve the same purpose in organizations. Stories are peopled with the heroes, the heroines, and the villains. They evoke values and explain the unwritten rules of engagement. They help us to make the link between what we do every day and where the business is headed. It's the antithesis of the long PowerPoint presentation packed with flow charts, figures, and tables, smart and glossy but barely memorable. Our stories need to be believable.

Middling Along—Don't Be a Mailbox

The challenge for the middle manager village is to add context and meaning to the messages coming from the top. This doesn't mean passing on what you just heard so that others hear the identical message. Think about it for a moment. The last time you heard some critical information coming down from the CEO's office, what did you do with it? It if was an e-mail, did you forward it on to key colleagues? If it was a presentation, did you share important slides with others? The core question is this: how did you help others make sense of the information and figure out how to apply it in their own jobs? The reason that the infamous information cascade becomes a trickle is that the farther it is from the source, the less meaning it has—unless all those involved see it as their role to add meaning as the information passes through their hands. This doesn't mean adding a personal interpretation or opinion or telling people what to do. It means helping others understand the context in which the decision was made or the approach was taken and then think through how it applies to them and how their tasks must adjust in response. If we pass on information but people don't change what they do as a result of the new information, then nothing changes. Strategy doesn't get executed.

The challenge for middle managers is often to believe that they have influence or importance in the execution chain. They are often neither executing the work nor making decisions about which work should be executed. Yet their role as translators is critical. At its simplest, the language of the executive team (a 15 percent increase in value-added sales to generation Y customers over the next 18 months) needs to make sense to those trying to make it happen ("In this region, in marketing we need to divert 23 percent of our budget immediately from targeting households run by 45–59-year-olds to messages directed to those ages 20–30."). Middle managers are critical in the communication loop passing intelligence and information, not just data, around the organization.

It's worth saying again. Every village has equal and different value at the Tump.

Reality Check from the Front Line
If the decision doesn't work in practice—that is, when people try to adjust their tasks in response and it doesn't work for

customers—well, that's important information to feed upward. The strategists and the executive team need a reality check from the front line on the feasibility of execution. If strategy, honestly pursued, really doesn't work in practice, then it's the wrong strategy. We need to work this out before our competition does, and so it's critical to make sure that there are effective mechanisms in place for upward feedback.[8]

How do you help people make sense of the execution journey and the demands it will place on them? How can they successfully identify and engage with all the messages and find ways to convert communication into real meaning? They need the space and the place to talk and engage. This means not just in formal, organized gatherings but in "their place" where they can test and argue and wrestle with subtleties. There is a need for debate. It's not about dissent; it's a process of interpretation that speeds us up and makes execution better. Through this process they reinterpret, reframe, and reposition your message to fit their reality. It makes the messages fit into their world and builds meaning as it is translated into the local dialect and examples.

As Peter Drucker so succinctly concludes, "The most important thing in communication is hearing what isn't said."[9]

Let the Villages Meet (or Where Is Our Tump?)

What we are discussing is a free flow of information and dialogue between the many villages in the organization so that all the villagers understand the role that their village must play in executing the strategy. The strategic fitness process[10] was developed at Harvard, and this process can be used to develop consensus on the organization's strategic direction. Conversations include whether there is the organizational capability to execute the strategy; how attitudes and behaviors are affecting performance; and the quality of leadership. The way it works is that the Elders have several meetings with a fitness task force of high-potential managers selected by them. Task force members interview 100 key executives (the Village) about the organization's effectiveness. The process of running these frank conversations increases dissatisfaction with the status quo and contributes to the urgency for change.

We have debate and dialogue across the organization and an increasing understanding of why and how we need to move forward. Let's now think about how we shift to widespread ownership and responsibility for executing the strategy.

Getting Ownership

Ideally, we are now in a position where the Elders have had the discipline to agree on four to five key priorities and to hold themselves accountable for them. They have tight and almost nonnegotiable guidelines for what is required so that they can monitor progress and performance and take action quickly if necessary. Further down the organization these rigidities have been relaxed as rules have become guidelines and regulations have become frameworks. The Elders and the Village of 100 have fixed the core principles, and everyone else has the space to flex and adjust to make the connections they need to make to get their work done in collaboration with others. We have achieved good commitment through experimentation, learning, and innovation rather than grudging compliance, repeated errors, and subversive cheating of the system. But more needs to be done. Everyone needs to understand his or her particular role in the game so that ownership is widespread across the business.

Let's understand some of the factors working for and against us.

Learned Helplessness Works Against Us

A colleague tells a story about empowerment that is visceral and therefore memorable.[11] He cites an experiment on dogs (if you are a dog lover, skip to the next paragraph—it's a graphic and horrible story). In these experiments, the aim is to test the dog's resilience and capacity for learning. The dog paces inside a cage shaped like a short corridor, with wire sides as well as a wire roof and bottom, that is, there is no escape. The first stage is to electrify one half of the cage. As the dog gets its first electric shock, it quickly learns to pace only to the halfway point in the cage and then turn back. The next stage in the experiment is to electrify instead the other half of the cage. The distressed dog quickly learns to avoid its original spot and to pace the other half of the cage. Finally the whole cage is electrified. The dog's reaction is at first violent, as it bounces around the cage trying to find a space free of pain. When it eventually realizes that there is no escape, it lies on the floor of the cage, whimpering. It has given up trying. It has learned to be helpless.

Obviously no one is going to get electrocuted into submission at work. But the mental equivalent can happen to us. It's not that we are physically damaged, but if we are told often enough that our opinion doesn't count, eventually we stop trying to put one forward. We become compliant, because no one is listening or cares, so it is no longer worthwhile to try to contribute. It's the equivalent of hanging our brain up on a peg by the door as we enter work (Henry Ford would have been delighted).[12]

We work with one company where there is a strong sense of hierarchy and respect for it. Executives have grades, that is, they are numbered in terms of seniority and therefore of importance. It's a competitive culture, where executives compete with each other and hold onto and exercise the power that they have. Unfortunately, it's become out of balance because respect for authority has turned into deference to it. The negative consequence is that people who run significant personal enterprises, in that they run households, families, and communities outside work, act in deferential and compliant ways at work. They ask permission and wait to be told. They are scared of making a mistake because of the repercussions it brings. They have learned to be helpless. This is a place where senior executives sign for water to be provided in meetings—not a good use of executive time.

You Have More Power Than You Think

How can the same people who act as responsible adults in their personal lives act like compliant children at work? Can it be different?

The truth is that, wherever you are in the hierarchy, you have power, too. It may not be the power of the title, or the executive suite, or your name on the door, but power comes from many sources. It comes from information and insight that you have; from expertise you hold; from contacts and your network and special relationships you have built; from experience; and from common sense. Too much focus on title and position as the sources of power and therefore of influence lead people to adopt a very narrow lens through which to view the world. There are intricacies of interdependence among human beings who are trying to make stuff happen, who are trying to execute the strategy. Those with the titles can't make it happen without everyone else coming along too.

Do Your Own Power Audit

"If you think you are too small to have an impact, try going to bed with a mosquito."[13] Understand the ways in which you rightfully have power and then exercise your power for the good of the whole. The problem with waiting to be told, or being given permission, is that you are withholding or underestimating what you have to offer. And in today's complex business environment, those who are most senior do not have all the answers or a monopoly on understanding the best way to turn. In fact, unless you help and guide them, they are likely to mess it up because of all the things that they don't and can't know.

Unless you acknowledge and use the power you have, you retreat into helplessness, as you see mistakes being made that you could have prevented if you had engaged. But you don't—you sit and wait to be told. And the senior executives then clamp down harder with detailed rules, and they listen even less as they try to avoid more mistakes in the future. People stick to the rules and avoid blame through blaming someone else, so accountability becomes diffuse and hard to pinpoint. Senior executives in turn feel increasingly isolated and unable to admit when they don't know the answer. As no one else is stepping forward, they feel as if they have to do so themselves, but they don't really have the insight or knowledge they need to fill the void which they themselves helped to create. Frustration increases, and effectiveness diminishes.

Get Fear Out of the System

It's a negative spiral and one in which everyone grows more frightened and more entrenched in position. Stress comes from feeling out of control. How can we get back in control and create options for ourselves so that we don't feel cornered?

In today's complex and turbulent world, it's impossible to make progress without making mistakes and learning from them. It is impossible to get it right the first time. With markets moving quickly, sometimes speed matters more, even though it's the enemy of getting things perfect. We need to get fear out of the system if we are going to be able to move fast, experiment, and learn.

Nick Forster, the former COO of Reed Exhibitions, is both a people person and an entrepreneur. In many senses, he sees these attributes as one and the same thing—his favorite job is to engage in conversation and help others feel confidence in new business ideas.[14] He finds the current business environment frustrating:

> People are afraid to make a move. I wish they would come up with more screwball ideas! But the quarterly statement drives us to be risk averse and the reward system doesn't help either. Short-termism in results and in the attitude of management stops people taking risks. Then increased regulation creates a restrictive, anti-risk culture. Because of the whole business environment, there is more fear in business today than there has been for quite some time.[15]

Forster has had a long and successful 40-year career and has reached the point of deciding to spend more time with his skis on.

Today he sees more fear of risk, more fear of failure, than he has seen for a long time. If he is right about the context, it means that we have to work even harder to encourage people to step forward and demand to be heard. We need to work against fear in the system because fear drives people to minimize risk by waiting to be told what to do. Fear works against experimentation and makes people reluctant to own what they do because of trepidation about the consequences of failure.

Ownership doesn't mean unbridled delegation to act at will. It is precisely the Elders' resolve in settling on four or five key strategic objectives that gives others the courage and the space to claim ownership because that ownership happens within well-defined parameters. People are more inclined to act on their own initiative if they understand clearly what is on, and what is off, the agenda. The challenge for the Elders is to have the will to set that bounded agenda. The agenda isn't additive. It doesn't mean a new set of five targets to be added to the previous list. It means agreeing to the five targets that replace, or take precedence over, everything else. It means agreeing to what to start and, probably even more critically, agreeing on what to stop.

Learn from Failure

There's another management game in which the facilitator uses a whistle to tell people when they make a wrong move and have to find a different way forward. Each time the whistle blows, the team is fined some of the money it has been allocated at the start of the game. What's interesting is how people react to the whistle. There are broadly two ways that teams tend to react. One way is to see it as a sign of failure, of having made a wrong move and so having to suffer a financial penalty. The other interpretation is that the whistle means the team has learned where not to go and therefore has learned the right way forward. The financial loss can be a good investment as it can help the team identify the way forward faster. It's pretty much the same in real life; there are those who see a mistake as a failure and those who see a mistake as an opportunity to learn fast and move faster.

Carol Dweck, a Stanford University psychologist, explains that learning is closely linked to our willingness to be open to and accepting of mistakes.[16] The outlook you adopt is also critical in determining whether you see risk as a normal part of business (and of life) or whether you see it as something to avoid. There is always a downside and an upside to risk, and it's more about getting the risk-reward ratio right than it is about avoiding risk altogether (hence the phrase, "Nothing ventured, nothing gained").

Nick Forster from Reed Exhibitions thinks risk aversion travels alongside the higher level of fear in business today. "There is too much emphasis on consequences—you need to add more conviction or belief to the mix. You need a no-blame culture, to take greater risks, because they lead to greater success. Great success can come if you can fail and learn from it. Senior executives don't let go, yet they are not the ones in touch with our customers—these are the people lower down and we should let them inform our strategy more."[17]

Forster sees the need for more bottom-up input into the strategy in order to make it more grounded and realistic. He is also arguing for creating a culture in which risks are encouraged and mistakes are seen as opportunities to learn, not as failure. It's essentially a culture of trust. When something goes wrong, it's not immediately assumed that someone must have acted in a thoughtless or stupid way. You trust your colleagues. So, instead, the assumption is that people are doing their best, but mistakes happen and instead of recriminations, we work together to analyze why and to avoid the same error in the future.

Can you do the same? How do you feel when the whistle blows?

Learn from Everything You Can

To find new ideas, Jeff Immelt, the chairman of GE, spends much of his time traveling and talking to customers, industry partners, government officials, and analysts.[18] Why does he do this? Because he is learning. Each of these stakeholders will bring a different angle to the same opportunity. Put those angles together, and you start to see a different pattern.

We regularly conduct sessions where executives talk to each other about successes and failures and share the characteristics of both with their colleagues. Simple questions are all it takes to elicit a lot of learning. Questions like, what was the situation, what happened, which questions did it make you ask yourself, what are the three things you would do differently next time? The value comes from sharing and from understanding that people from different functions, geographies, and businesses can find common lessons. The patterns are there if you take the time to stop and look for them. And learning helps you to avoid disappointment next time around through repeating the same mistake.

Employees build real ownership through self-directed change—where they are given the space to debate, decide, and act, as long as they collaborate with others in the process (there is no point in doing something that works for you if it causes problems for another part of the business). They deliver more—because they want to, not because leaders have demanded it. We need to stop paying lip service to the contributions that people can make without any supervision.

"People Are Our Most Important Asset"

The phrase, "People are our most important asset" is in quotation marks for a reason. It's a phrase that passes for an in-joke in corporate circles. It is as maligned as the much-used phrase in the glossily published annual report that is not lived out in practice. It is a world in which people are overplanned and underled, with more head than heart. As one executive explained, "We say we put people first, but we are perfuming a pig. Google give employees free meals and nap-pods. We don't even give our employees a free cup of coffee. They come third, right after our stamping machines and robots." Executives know intellectually that if no one showed up for work tomorrow, the organization would cease to exist. Yet often workers are not at the top of the leadership to-do list. They are frequently superseded by customers or shareholders or even by leaders doing the work themselves. Yet think about how we could transform our business if we truly believed our own rhetoric. If our mindset is genuinely that our people are more important than anything else, it changes radically how we approach work. As another executive explained, "We don't get customer-first right because we don't get employee-first right."

It can be done. A small number of businesses worldwide put the much-quoted truism into powerful practice, businesses like Southwest Airlines, Google, Apple, and Virgin. Virgin's check-in staff members outside London's Heathrow are supplied by an agency, so you may sometimes see them in one airline livery at one time of day and then in Virgin's red uniform at others. Virgin is great at making people feel involved and has a real talent for celebration. Agency staff members feel measurably more engaged with Virgin than when they don another airline's uniform.

A Cat May Look at a King[19]

Businesses that are good at engaging their staff include Claridges, a luxury hotel in Mayfair, London, where Thomas Kochs is its youngest ever general manager. We took a behind-the-scenes look at how the hotel delivers a top-class experience for its guests. To put this luxury hotel into context, one of its managers has a story that he likes to tell. "People used to ring up the telephone operators here," says Timothy Lock, "and they would ask: 'Could I speak to the king?' and the operator would reply, 'Which one?'" The average cost of an overnight stay is about £600, but celebrities can spend up to £6,000 if they insist, as some of them do, on having their suite redecorated for their stay. Over the past 150 years, Claridges has played host to hundreds of heads of state and is informally known as the annex to Buckingham Palace (the British Queen's London residence).

We worked with Claridges from the end of 2012 and heard many more inside stories from Thomas Kochs. He runs an information-gathering system on guests that would make the CIA or MI5 (or any other government intelligence gathering agency) proud. Each member of the staff gathers snippets of information on guests which is then stored in a personal file so that when the guests return, everything is in place as they like it, right down to the type of water they prefer in the minibar and which side of the bed they sleep on. There's no point in burdening employees who are running around the hotel all day with having to find a computer to log in the information. They simply pick up a phone, dial a special number, and leave a voice mail with the information. Daily briefings ensure that everyone has access to the guest insights that have been logged, so guests can be greeted on arrival and daily with enquiries about their family members, friends, and pets. The room is made up just as they like it, furniture moved to their favorite positions, and room accessories added for a highly customized touch.

Kochs is absolutely clear about the pecking order—employees come first. The hotel deliberately hires people who are sensitive and who have a good intuition about people—good EQ. In fact, Kochs goes so far as to say that while a background in hospitality is desirable, he's prepared to train the right people from scratch. This hotel hosts heads of state and royalty at a steady rate, but the Claridges' philosophy is clear. Without the employees and their dedicated and refined data gathering activities and their exquisite attention to detail, the service that differentiates Claridges would not be delivered. It is only through putting employees first that Claridges comes first for its customers, its guests. And the employees know that. They know that the hotel relies on them and sees them as central to the business, which gives them a sense of pride and a sense of ownership.

From Hotels to Beer

Not every business is a service business, so let's take a manufacturing example. August Anheuser Busch III (known as Triple Sticks) is a great-grandson of Anheuser-Busch founder Adolphus Busch and was the U.S. brewing company's chairman from 1977 until November 30, 2006. Previously he served as president of the Anheuser-Busch Companies (ABC) from 1974 until June 2002 and chief executive officer of ABC from 1975 until June 2002. He had a reputation for absolute dedication to quality. One apocryphal story tells of the time he pulled over one of the large delivery trucks transporting beer (in a snow storm) because he thought that it was too dirty and so a poor representative for the brand. He was careful to make quality everyone's priority, not just his. He wanted everyone to own it. Another story is about him stopping the production line—a huge and costly decision in a continuous manufacturing operation—because he thought the printing on the cans wasn't up to standard. He told a production employee: "It's your job to stop the line when the quality isn't good enough." He couldn't be the eyes of the business everywhere, and he wanted everyone to feel the passion that he felt as an owner.

It can be done.

By now, we should have widespread understanding of and felt ownership for strategy execution. But we can't simply rely on everybody to do the right thing all the time. Let's think about the third part in our trilogy of communications, ownership, and follow-through and consider how we now embed it into the system for consistent performance.

Follow-Through

Dominique Fournier, the former CEO of Infineum, is committed to follow-through. "After you reached a negotiated commitment, you stuck to it and delivered. We were not extremist or dogmatic, but when you are changing the culture, people look to see how you react when the required behavior is not delivered. If every time people fail you treat it as if it's OK, then failure becomes OK. We insisted on accountability, rigor and challenge. We created standards of organizational excellence in order to unleash latent capability."[20] Fournier follows through to set the tone for a performance-oriented culture, but he also does it to unleash the potential in people.

In a world where much of what we have taken for granted seems to be changing dramatically, from weather patterns to how to recover from an economic recession (many commentators are confounded by Japan's lost 20 years), it's almost as though executives have developed attention deficit disorder (ADD).[21] In the face of unpredictable change and market pressure for short-term gains, executives keep changing the rules in response, and strategy endures for less and less time. One crisis has barely passed before another one looms, needing a new set of responses. And the new rules tend to be additive, without enough attention being paid to what to take off the shopping list, to make space for the new items. We issue orders and communications but seem to lack the time or the will to circle back to check for understanding or to see whether what we asked for has actually been executed.

For real ADD, stimulants like Ritalin, Adderall, and Dexedrine are prescribed in order to increase dopamine levels in the brain. Dopamine is a neurotransmitter associated with motivation, pleasure, attention, and movement. For many people with ADD or ADHD, stimulant medications boost concentration and focus while reducing hyperactive and impulsive behaviors. Can we find the organizational equivalent of Ritalin to help us to extend our attention span and stop us from being so jumpy?

The Internet Fuels ADD

The Internet isn't helping focus or concentration. It's chopping ideas into nanosecond sound bites, and some people believe that it is even making us stupid. Nicholas Carr has written a book that essentially suggests this.[22] There is plenty of research to demonstrate that our brains cannot cope with the constant stimulus of new information and that we operate at a level of heightened stress on a continuous basis. Because the stress is continuous, we fail to notice it. Carr demonstrates, for example, that the Internet encourages rapid sampling of small bits of information from many sources but that on our surfing journeys we may end up forgetting why we started in the first place. (It's a bit like going upstairs to get something and forgetting what you wanted to get—although this analogy won't work for younger readers.) So we are becoming more adept at scanning but losing our capacity for concentration and reflection.

Churn, Not Change

The danger is that if we start many new initiatives without completing them, we are encouraging churn rather than change. What does this mean? GE, the global company that has a finance business as well as manufacturing appliances, lighting, and power systems for business and domestic use, is famous for educating employees at its training facility called Crotonville. Crotonville is GE's global leadership institute, founded in 1956, the world's first major corporate university. The 59-acre main campus in New York state hosts thousands of GE employees and customers each year. Thousands more attend Crotonville leadership courses around the world. Over its lifespan, it has created leading ideas and concepts through collaboration with numerous academics and gifted practitioners. One such concept is a six-step method for looking at how to lead and embed change.

We have used this tool many times to help companies diagnose how they are leading change. It's fascinating—and helpful—when you uncover a consistent fail point, that is, one step in the guide where the change agenda fails time and time again. It's what distinguishes companies that are adept at seeing change through from those where people feel tired and under constant pressure—where churn, rather than change, is the order of the day. "Change" is where something new is launched and successfully embedded. "Churn" is where initiatives are started but aren't followed through, and so they fail to stick. Because things start but don't stick, another initiative will be launched in another attempt to change. It becomes an exhausting cycle of start, falter, try again, and falter again. Employees lose a sense of meaning in their work because they don't reach the point of psychological closure of a job or project completed.

Where's the Ritalin?

Getting rid of ADD means building a true orientation for performance where the focus is on outcomes, not activities, and where simple measures act both as scorecards and as warning systems. We worked with an investment bank that had a performance management system based on a forced distribution. A forced distribution means that the manager has to allocate his or her reports into a number of categories, with an agreed-upon percentage allocated to each category. In this case, the bank had four classes of performance. Class A denoted exceptional performance; class B, above average performance; class C, the performance expected of a professional in the role; and a class D ranking meant that the individual needed development. Obviously, the intent was that most employees would fall into class C—the level of performance widely expected of a professional.

Sadly, the performance management system wasn't working and hadn't worked for the 20 years it had been in place. As a result, 90 percent of employees ended up in categories A and B. Is this bank unusual? Not really. Most managers dislike a forced distribution system, for a variety of reasons. One is that the manager doesn't want to demotivate people by allocating them to a low ranking; managers dislike the transparency (everyone knows the ranking they receive, because it is recorded); and sometimes the manager really has a small team of gifted people, so a forced distribution feels unfair when everyone is operating at the same (high) level. Well, it was crunch time. After 20 years, the good times were coming to an end, and the bank was going to have to reduce in size and make some people redundant. How would they decide whom to keep and whom to let go, when for the last 20 years the managers had consistently declared 90 percent of the workforce to be above average or exceptional?

It turned out to be pretty easy. We asked them to put the name of every person they managed onto an individual Post-it note and then to stick the names on the wall in roughly three categories; must keep, negotiable, and can be let go. Unlike the formal performance management system, 90 percent did not make it into the "must keep" category. The managers allocated about 10 percent of employees each into the "must keep" and "can be let go" categories, leaving 80 percent in the "negotiable" category. It took about seven and a half minutes to complete. (Just out of interest, we compared the results with the last three years' performance reviews—no match.) So managers know how to measure performance—they just need to be motivated to do it.

Build a Performance Orientation

A performance orientation has three aspects. The first is that managers like the performance management system, whatever it is, and so are prepared to use it; the second is to understand and truly believe that recognition is widely underused as a way of encouraging performance; and last that we need to measure achievement, not activity.

We discuss above how managers won't use a performance management system if they don't like it or believe in it or if it gives them problems with relationships. The challenge with having, but not properly using, a performance management system is that you end up with the worst of all possible worlds. High achievers are demotivated because their performance fails to distinguish them if everyone is lumped into the above average category, and, by the same token, low achievers aren't motivated to try harder. Managers fail to pay attention to what should be happening—regular conversations about performance, development, and progress—and instead end up checking off boxes in haste, once a year, when the human resources department wants the paperwork submitted.

The outcome is that what goes on an individual's record doesn't necessarily represent his or her performance. What we end up with, strangely, is mediocrity, because managers tolerate acceptable levels of underperformance. Managers put up with performance that is just about okay, because they estimate that it's probably not worth the effort of trying to push it higher. This builds apathy and inertia. Why try if the colleague next to me doesn't? It infects the execution process—it slows us down. We look at the role of voice in creating ownership in Chapter 2. It's the same here. Let your managers loose on designing the performance management system. It may not be perfect, but better an imperfect system that gets used than a perfect one that gets only rote responses. And manage the performance of the performance management system. There should be accolades and penalties for managers who do and don't play the game.

The Right, Not the Ritual

Real performance management means regular, ongoing conversations with people about how they are doing and where they need to change, develop, and grow. There is so much research that reminds us over and over again of how important regular recognition is to motivation.[23] Yet we overlook or ignore this advice by claiming that we are too busy to meet regularly to discuss performance or that people are adults and should just be left to get on with it. Yet recognition has been proven to increase motivation and improve financial results. If we asked you if you were too busy to improve the financial performance of your company, you'd think we were crazy. Yet that's exactly what every manager is doing every time she or he fails to make time for a performance conversation.

Put it on the calendar—and make it stick.

Achievements

We all know that a résumé or curriculum vitae should list achievements, not just activities that the person undertook, in order to maximize the chance of getting a new job. It's the same with performance on the job. We work with one organization where managers described to us the best way to get on and get ahead. "What you have to do is rush around and looked stressed and busy." They felt general dissatisfaction with the performance management system, "Because it rewards smoke and mirrors, not real achievement." Everyone knows the charade they are playing, and it's demotivating. If people are rewarded for what they achieve, then you can spend less time worrying about how they did it (as long as it's within the framework of your values and ethics), leaving them more freedom to get done what needs to be done. You won't be tempted to waste time interfering in processes that you may not fully understand, and they will feel trusted and empowered.

Goal Setting

Jeremy Pelczer, ex-CEO of Thames Water, offers some advice on the goal setting process. "There is a big difference between fear of failure and the courage and bravery to strive for stretch targets. Grade the targets (conservative, likely, stretching but achievable and heroic) and then have honest conversations about how big is the gap and what changes in capacity and capabilities are needed to bridge the gap. Don't tell people what to do, partly because there are lots of places where they can excuse themselves and explain failure and partly because the sense of achievement is all the greater if they work out what is needed."[24] Regardless of how the target is agreed upon, Pelczer suggests that it also needs to be accompanied by an honest conversation about whether the individual is capable of achieving it and what further support or development might be needed. It's sage advice about making no assumptions that the target will automatically be met. It's also an argument for joint goal setting rather than telling people what to do.

To measure achievement rather than activity, you need to be able to set goals with your direct reports. Research tells us that setting specific goals (such as, I want to earn $500 more a month) generates higher levels of performance than setting general goals (such as, I want to earn more money), and that goals that are hard to achieve are linearly and positively connected to performance.[25] The more challenging the goal (as long as it's not unrealistic), the more a person will persist and work to reach it, so goal setting can move an individual from low to high performance. The sense of achievement is very satisfying.

However, there are two conditions that can intervene—feedback (people need to know how they are doing) and acceptance (the person accepts and believes in the goal). Joint goal setting by the supervisor and direct report working together leads to higher commitment than just telling someone what to do. Interestingly, it doesn't lead to higher commitment than if the supervisor provides a convincing rationale for a goal that he or she simply assigns to someone. So if you want to set a goal for someone, go ahead, but make sure that the person really accepts it. A goal that is clearly linked to the overall mission of the organization will have more meaning for the individual (see Chapter 3), and hard or stretching goals help a person to persist. But how do we make sure that we are really measuring achievement, not activity?

Measures, Soft and Hard

The final piece in the performance management puzzle is making sure that you measure the right things in the right way. The trick is to go for simple yet comprehensive measures. Think about your measurement system like the dashboard of a car, rather than the cockpit of a plane. In the airplane cockpit, you are faced with myriad flashing lights, which work well for diagnosing any slight fault in a complex system, but which work less well for setting general overall direction. The car dashboard, on the other hand, keeps measurements few, simple, and clear—how fast you are going, how much fuel is left, and whether your lights are on or not. Easier to read quickly and so easier to make decisions about direction and pace. So keep the measures few in number and simple in form.

That said, you want your few indicators to measure both short- and long-term achievement. We all know that a lot can be achieved over the short term at the expense of the long term. For example, you could throw a year's budget at one aspect of your work, so that one project would succeed, but at the expense of others starting later in the year. This is a microcosm of the perennial challenge to satisfy the short-term exigencies of the market while at the same time putting aside enough investment for the long-term prosperity of the organization. And equally, it's advisable to use hard and soft measures of success, that is, quantitative and qualitative measures. The obvious clash here could be between financial and cultural measures. If you are measured only on financial indicators, you could achieve your results at the expense of appropriate and respectful behavior toward others. Looked at from the other side, if you are measured only on acting appropriately, your financial contribution to the company goal might be diminished, as you focus on the "how" more than on the "what." So hard and soft measures can complement each other and keep you safely on the good performance tightrope balanced between the two.

Never Say Never[26]

To create a culture for execution, you need communication, ownership, and follow-through. No aspect on its own is sufficient, but follow-through is particularly important. If you present idea after idea and don't check back consistently, it is likely that the ideas won't come to fruition. You will become frustrated and wonder why "they can't just get the job done." The people who work for you will accuse you of "initiative-itis" and of "moving the goalposts." No one's a winner. A culture for execution requires consistency and discipline—you can't give up.

Let's see if we can pull a culture of execution together in a real business story.

The context is Great Britain in the 1990s. For readers who aren't old and aren't British, it's hard to imagine the legacy of industrial strife and militancy that Britain was living in back then. The 1970s was a horrific decade, a period of rampant inflation and public sector strikes. Trash went uncollected on the streets, a hazard to health, there were oil shortages resulting from the 1973 oil crisis, and industrial action by coal miners led to a three-day working week in 1973–1974, as electricity supply was limited. Those who wanted to work longer hours did so by candlelight. This Britain was a long way from the Britain that led the Industrial Revolution and dominated the European and world economy during the nineteenth century. Electing a Labour Government in 1974 led to an uneasy truce with trade unions, which broke down again in 1978. The extreme industrial strife along with rising inflation and unemployment led Britain to be nicknamed the "sick man of Europe." Margaret Thatcher was voted in as Conservative prime minister in 1979 and spent the 1980s working to reduce the power of the trade unions.

Author Simon Carter was CEO of Baxi Heating, a long-established business manufacturing domestic central heating boilers and gas fires in the early 1990s. Baxi had been a family-owned firm for more than 130 years and more recently an employee-owned partnership. In all that time, there had been no industrial relations breakdowns or strikes. The company had always had trade unions, but negotiations were benign in the good years. The unions would turn up every April with a laundry list, and management had the money to meet their demands in exchange for productivity improvements. But by the late 1980s, the company was drifting—confronting new technologies, market structure changes, and increased competition from strong European players. Carter and the Elders devised a radical turnaround strategy to increase operational effectiveness and to deliver renewed focus on customers. On January 1, 1990, the company improvement plan was launched to get the business out of trouble. The Village had been consulted. The organization was delayered and old silo-style functions were replaced by customer-facing business units.

The 1990 pay negotiations dragged on for weeks. On one side, management was talking about how the company needed to change to survive. On the other side, the unions were insisting on no change to the agreement informally known as "jobs in company," that is, no compulsory redundancies. This was the legacy left by the previous 20 years of union militancy in the United Kingdom, which hadn't touched Baxi until now. By 1990, Baxi could no longer justify the wage bill, and redundancies were announced. In response, the workforce voted for industrial action.

Ronnie Bootle was a shop steward at Baxi at the time. He recalls management meetings after the redundancies and the return to work. "The first few meetings were horrible. I couldn't look at the management at first—I had lost heart. I had always been involved in promoting education in the workplace and I knew better than most management that we had a literacy problem on the shop floor. After all the trauma of the layoffs which cut right through the old company culture, I wanted to know if this management really cared about its people in the way they alleged, so I decided to test them. I proposed literacy education through training courses for colleagues on the shop floor and Simon agreed. That started to rebuild my trust."

The delayering had restructured the organization into self-managed teams of 8–10 people, in support of a renewed focus on customers. These teams were allowed to make any changes they wanted to improve working practices. For example, the paint shop workers completely changed the way to paint the products. Bootle remembers one character especially. "Across the company we had people whose sole job was to keep the place clean, tidy and safe. One of these guys had learnt how to read and write through the literacy program and after spending a lifetime of saying nothing much to anybody, now we couldn't stop him writing letters to all and sundry, management works committees, safety groups, you name it, with recommendations for improvement. The thing is, you could see things happening when you asked for change, so you wanted to keep making suggestions. It was infectious and built a huge momentum behind the new way of working. My team even consolidated all our working hours into four long days, so that we only worked from Monday to Thursday."

There was more. For years the unions had asked for financial and other information to understand how the company was doing, but it had always been denied. Now Carter made it available to them. Bootle recalls: "We had always asked for full information and never got it. Now we had it and we soon realized we couldn't make head nor tail of it! We had to go on courses to understand it and once we did, we were more realistic in our pay negotiations. The Negotiating Committee didn't ask for a pay rise at the annual negotiations in April for the next two years—we could see that an idiotic pay rise would cost jobs."

Baxi was turned around, through a process of communication, with open and transparent access to financial data; and ownership, through self-managed teams empowered to make decisions; and follow-through, with a fully implemented performance management system. If you have access to the BBC Archives, you can see TV footage covering the company in late 1991, because the company was so successful in its transformation. Was the result an energized culture for execution?

Bootle believes so. "Empowered is a word that's used too loosely. At Baxi, as long as you met your targets, you really were empowered to do anything you wanted. The whole workforce got behind building the new organization. It was a pleasure to go to work."

The turnaround took two years. Even with lots of small wins and celebrations along the way, it's still a long time to sustain the effort for continuous improvement. In the next chapter, we look at how to build endurance for the long haul of execution and successful change.

Summary

In this chapter we define exactly a culture of execution; a place of communication, ownership, and follow-through. The irony is that we talk a lot about the importance of communication and then too often fail to communicate. We need the right kind of communication. This isn't about tablets of wisdom being cascaded down the hierarchy. The phrase "cascade briefing" should be banned because it has overtones of one-way communication and a sense that the top of the organizational pyramid needs to instruct the rest. No wonder the cascade withers quickly to a dribble.

We see the organization as a collection of villages beyond the Elders and top 100 Village. Each has its special role and part to play in strategy execution, and each has unique and critical information that must be shared in order for execution to succeed. In today's busy and complex business world, people can lose sight of the strategy and their role in it. They start to believe that they are powerless to assist or to resist. Ownership comes through encouraging experiments and allowing people the space to fail and to learn how to execute better.

And finally, we suggest that leaders have a bad case of attention deficit disorder. Through consistent, deliberate follow-through, what gets measured actually will get done. We will improve and speed up the process for strategy execution.

So far, we have mobilized the Village, gathered the Elders, and created an organization where people understand its purpose and find meaning in work every day. They feel energized and capable of taking independent action. But we are not quite done. Execution is a marathon, not a sprint. Our fifth and final step is to get into training for the marathon.

5

Build Endurance

I have a lot of stamina and I have a lot of resilience.
—Hillary Clinton

Webster's definition of *stamina* is "staying power, endurance." Endurance is the ability to sustain a prolonged stressful effort or activity, like running a marathon. Hillary Clinton is right. To be successful in today's 24/7 world, we need endurance to meet all the demands we face each and every day—to stay on track until the strategy is executed.

To endure sounds, frankly, a bit grim. Yet the truth is that, in business today, we are asking people to sustain a high level of continuous effort. If strategy has become a sprint, as leaders lurch from each economic crisis to the next social unrest, then strategy execution has become a marathon. Getting the organization to refocus on the customer, or developing the capabilities to expand globally, or starting a new business line all take time to become established. In fact, it's not so much about running just one marathon but a series of marathons, one right after the other. It's an endurance sport.

And there is no option. As Sir Jeremy Greenstock notes, "Institutions fade in their effectiveness when there is a long period of peace, without change. They get to the point where they are beyond redeeming themselves and so their effectiveness reduces."[1]

Strategy Has Become a Sprint

Even the most traditional of organizations no longer seems to have a 5-year strategy. The horizon has shrunk to about 18 months, to last just long enough until the next market nosedive and the executive reaction to it. At the same time, execution has become the long game. It can take years to embed a truly customer-focused orientation or to become a global organization. Everyone is trying to sustain the energy to play consistently enough and long enough, and senior executives are struggling with their new role as marathon trainers. It's as John Chambers, the charismatic CEO of Cisco, says: "Operational execution trumps innovation."[2] It's a follow-through game.

A Sidebar on Getting Strategy Back, or Getting Back to Strategy

This book is about how to execute a strategy, not about how to get the right strategy in the first place. But it's worth pausing to think about whether, and if, we can get back to strategy as we have known it in the past—as a long-term proposition. Today, market volatility means that many leaders are arguing for strategy as a weapon of short-term opportunism. Tom Albanese, until 2013 the CEO of the global mining giant Rio Tinto, has a different vision. It's about returning to a 20-year-plus strategy horizon. Mining, like many capital-intensive industries, works to decade-long cycles. After World War II, growth was driven by the United States, Europe, and Japan. After the 2008 global economic slump, growth has been driven primarily by BRIC (Brazil, Russia, India, China—sometimes adding S for South Africa or K for South Korea) and other emerging economies. The long-term, underlying trend is currently upwards. An investment in mining can take three years to build and five years to establish itself. Meanwhile, the market (analysts and investors) pays attention to business cycle noise, so investors advise stopping growth or advancing growth as they see the next up- or downturn coming—the short-term business ups and downs. This advice is always too late for mining, which cannot move fast enough. It's not good for the business. The result is twofold. In the long term, supply is always behind or ahead of demand—miners are exuberant when they are running to build supply in order to catch up with demand and despairing when they are trying to cut back on oversupply. In the short term, the result is a sawtooth effect, as they yank the business around to try to adjust faster.

Albanese advises, "Because the market pays attention to business cycle noise, there is an increased level of volatility, whose amplitude is higher and frequency is greater, making it harder to execute consistently a long term strategy than in the past. We need to pay attention to the underlying trends and not to the short term swings."[3]

It's No Fun

It's a brave CEO who goes against investor advice, but the fact is that investors are pressing companies to change faster than is effective for the long-term good of the business. They overreact to market signals, resulting in the sawtooth effect and short-term volatility. It's really hard to get people engaged with a strategy and execute it if you change it year after year, or sometimes even faster than that. Albanese is right. Strategy needs to get back to vision and a focus on sustainability for prosperity in the longer term. Focusing on near-term market gains drives business to sprint for short-term growth, which may not be sustainable or even necessary. And it's getting to the point where it's not just hard on the people trying to execute; it's too hard. There is a great number of exhausted people in business today.

Pressure means that strategy has become code for 12 hours of root canal work. Stefan Stern, a management writer and visiting professor at Cass Business School in London, expresses it in even more extreme terms: "Whether through fear, or lack of confidence, or bitter experience—some managers find strategy too awful to contemplate. It has become an arid, joyless affair, predictably grim and predictably disappointing."[4]

Somewhat disturbing sidebar over, let's get back to execution.

Marathon Endurance[5]

Not everyone is Eddie Izzard. Eddie Izzard is a British stand-up comedian, actor, and writer, who in 2009 completed 43 marathons in 51 days for the charity Sport Relief, despite having no prior history of long-distance running. It was an astonishing achievement. Most mortals are frailer and need a lot of support and encouragement to reach the finish line of even one marathon. So let's think about what it takes to run a marathon for real and then translate the lessons back into organizational life.

Running a marathon requires mental strength as much as it does physical fitness, and each part of the marathon has its own mental challenges. How you start determines how—and if—you finish. Always, always, always start out slow. With any luck, you will have put in the training hours you need, and so when you start your marathon, you'll feel strong and confident. More than that, it's exciting. As you stand on the starting line (or more accurately, as you shuffle forward to the starting line with thousands of other runners), the crowd will be cheering and all the runners will be a bit nervous, eager to set off as soon as the starting signal sounds. You must keep telling yourself to hold back—you are in this for the long haul. If you start out too fast, you will exhaust yourself in the early stages of the race. The best-case scenario will then be that you have a miserable end to the race, feeling dreadful and constantly unsure whether you can find the stamina to keep going. The worst-case scenario will be that you will fail to finish at all (statistically, this happens to less than 2 percent of us, so, just like Woody Allen says, 80 percent of success is just turning up—apparently 98 percent, when it comes to the marathon). Run your own marathon. Don't be worried if you see a lot of people passing you. Remember the tortoise and the hare? They may be starting out way too fast, so you'll catch them later, at your own pace. Have confidence in yourself.

Chunk It Up

Don't get too emotional. It's tempting to start taking ice cream and sweets from spectators and jumping up and down when you pass family members and friends. Try to stay as calm as possible; you'll need to conserve your mental energy for the rest of the race. Celebrate the small wins—each mile marker is another mile closer to victory.

From the midpoint onward in the race, break up the marathon into smaller segments. It will make the distance feel more manageable. At mile 17, for example, think,: "One six mile race, then it's just 0.2 of a mile to finish." Never forget that the exact distance is 26.2 miles—it's amazing how impossible that last 0.2 mile can feel if you have prepared mentally for only the first 26! Stay mentally tough. Your mental toughness will really start to be tested during the last miles. Don't give in to periods of self-doubt and discomfort. Remember all the preparation that you have done and have faith in it. Think about how hard you have worked and how rewarding it will be to complete your marathon.

Beat Boredom

Amazingly, boredom can be one of the biggest mental challenges to accompany the physical challenge. Do whatever it takes to keep your mind occupied: sing songs, play mental games, count people, talk to other runners. Increasingly, today's runners listen to music or even phone friends for a chat. From mile 21 onward, as you approach the end of the race, think outside the body. Chances are you'll be feeling a little bit of pain and discomfort during these miles. You will certainly feel tired. Let your mind take over from your body and try to focus on the outside—the spectators, the signs, the other runners, the scenery. Set smaller milestones between the mile markers. Start counting down the miles and the minutes. Take all the encouragement that you can from spectators—wearing a vest with your name on it pays huge dividends as they shout out your name with words of encouragement. Talk to yourself and continuously tell yourself how well you are doing. Don't let yourself start feeling unable or helpless (remember the story about learned helplessness from Chapter 4?).

At this point in the race, you need to dig down deep for extra strength. Remind yourself of what you've sacrificed to get to this point. Remember how you've worked through fatigue during your training runs and how you can now do it again, one more time. And finally, as you cross that finish line—don't stop! Keep moving, keep walking, keep talking—just stop running. Feel good about your achievement, whether you made the race time you had set for yourself or not. You've done it—what a victory, what an amazing accomplishment. No one can ever take it away from you.

Running the Strategy Execution Marathon

Without stretching the analogy too far, what similarities are there with running a marathon and the marathon of strategy execution at work? The first piece of advice is to be fit for the race. What does training look like in the context of strategy execution? There are two levels of readiness—one is for you as an individual and the other is organizational.

Put in the Training

Ali Gill, the former Olympic rower and lover of extreme sports (Arctic marathon running), knows a lot about endurance training.

She advises, "It's all about building your base. You want it as wide as is physiologically possible, so that you can build your pyramid as high as possible. It's about endless and sustained repetition, not sudden bursts. It takes at least four years to be able to cope with the level of training you need to achieve elite status. When building the base, there are lots of things going on around you. It's easy to be distracted by short-term promises of results and you need to zone out and focus on keeping doing only the things which build that broad base for you."[6]

This is why elite status is so hard to achieve. If you like keeping fit and active but struggle to find time to sustain three outings a week, can you imagine the concentrated effort and determination it takes to get out there every day and put in the hours?

It's about practicing, practicing, practicing existing skills. Take communicating as a leader, our first touchstone in creating a culture of execution in Chapter 4. To achieve elite status, you need to zone out the noise in the system and just keep doing it. You think you have consulted everyone, but people keep coming back with the same questions. You think you have explained it a thousand times, but people still don't seem to get it. Instead of becoming frustrated, see yourself as an elite athlete operating at a higher level of skill. The more you practice communication, the better you become at it. It's the ones who get out only two or three times a week who struggle and get frustrated. Whether it's communicating, or leading change, or motivating others, just keep putting in the hours of endurance training that achieve elite status. Without the right training, you won't be fit for the long race.

The Elders will be pretty focused on building fresh organizational capabilities to cope with new circumstances and demands. They will hire the expertise and skills, if they can't find them internally, to build the enhanced organization necessary to execute the strategy. So make sure you get the training you need to stay current, even if you are not going for elite status.

Run the Race

Now let's look at some analogies with running the race itself. "Don't start out too fast" translates well into work. If you set unrealistic goals, you will disappoint yourself and others, and we need the opposite feeling, one of steady progress. There are a lot of people with Type A personalities[7] in leadership positions— ambitious, organized, stretched, and keen to help others, who take on more than they can handle, who are impatient and proactive. People with Type A personalities are often high-achieving "workaholics" who multitask, push themselves with deadlines, and hate both delays and ambivalence. This can make them demanding and impatient for success. If you recognize yourself here, learn to pace yourself. Keep reminding yourself that it's not a sprint and that you need to conserve energy to keep on going, day after day. Develop tortoise-like capabilities rather than be hare-brained.

There is an amusing greeting card that depicts a crowd of people chanting: "What do we want? Gratification. When do we want it—now!" The desire for instant gratification can work against long-term, steady achievement of strategic goals. This is linked to the marathon running analogy of "Don't get too emotional," and, "Have confidence in yourself." What we are really talking about here is emotional intelligence, which we cover in Chapter 3. Part of emotional intelligence is about our ability to empathize with others, but another important aspect is about self-control. It's about mental toughness and confidence. Manage yourself so that you can lead others. Keep your eye on the long-term, bigger prize (crossing that line), and move toward it steadily. In running, as in life, pacesetters don't win the race. Don't sprint and run out of energy in a heap of early disappointment.

Midpoint Transition

"From the midpoint onwards, break it up into smaller segments." The midpoint is catalytic in any project. Connie Gersick found in her research that any project work group decides and agrees on an approach pretty quickly.[8] (This is in contrast to the prevailing view up until that time that groups go through four standard stages of form, storm, norm, and perform in building the team and deciding how to approach a task.[9]) The group sticks with this approach until the halfway point, that is, the moment halfway between the first meeting and the task deadline. At this moment, there is a concentrated explosion of changes, as the group drops old patterns, adopts new perspectives, and makes dramatic progress.

It's a major transition point. Therefore, halfway through any strategy execution project, expect a reorientation of thinking and approach. It's not just English football that's a game of two halves (we see how often the game can change radically in the second half). See it as an expected adjustment rather than be dismayed or worried that you are offtrack. This isn't to say that your strategy changes or that it's the only adjustment point. Strategy execution is a bit like driving on a long journey. Getting from point A to point B is never a straight line; there are roadblocks, rerouting because of roadwork or closures, and varying amounts of traffic. The driver is alert and vigilant, looking out for changing road signals and directions. In addition, halfway through your journey, it's time to refocus attention, check progress against the plan, and tighten attention on shorter-term targets. There is an apocryphal story of a CEO who established an 18-month deadline at an executive team meeting. Two months later the group met again and someone mentioned the 18-month deadline. The CEO corrected his colleague; "No, it's 16 months now." It is easy to fall into the trap of quoting deadlines that somehow get stuck in a time warp.[10] Keep up the pressure, one mile at a time, and don't lose sight of the mile counter.

Breaking it up into smaller segments also sounds like classic management advice. Remember "Celebrate the small wins" from Chapter 3? While creating a strategy is the job of a small number of people—the CEO and his or her Elders—strategy execution is the work of thousands. If your job generally requires you to think only weeks ahead, keeping going toward a three- to five-year target will be much easier if you can celebrate short-term, periodic goals reached en route to the final target.[11]

Supersize Yourself

One final idea. You know how some fast food outlets ask, "Can I supersize that for you?" when you place a food order? What they are asking is if you would like the portion sizes to be larger. How about supersizing yourself; that is, regularly tell yourself how well you are doing. This may sound a bit contrived, but it will keep your confidence and resolve intact. Charles Darwin suggested in 1872 that emotional responses influence our feelings. "The free expression by outward signs of an emotion intensifies it," he wrote.[12] So if you are happy and you smile or laugh, it intensifies your feeling of happiness.[13] Even more than that, smiling when you're unhappy has been clinically proven to improve mood.[14] Reminding yourself of what you have done well is known to increase your feelings of self-efficacy, or confidence in a specific task. You are running the strategy execution marathon one step at a time, and every step taken is another step nearer the finish line and victory. It's good to keep reminding yourself that you are doing well.

So there are many parallels between running a physical race and the marathon of strategy execution. Of course, the multiple moving parts that must be aligned during strategy execution in a complex business situation are a far greater intellectual challenge than the game plan for running a marathon. For a start, in a marathon, individuals run their own race, and all the advice is geared toward the individual. To execute a strategy, the whole running field has to be coordinated. To the individual challenges of mental and physical endurance we add alignment, as people need to avoid tripping each other up or somehow sabotaging someone else's race.

But the principles for keeping going for the long haul still apply; train for the race, keep a steady pace, celebrate the milestones, and keep mentally strong. Let's dig a little deeper into how we can develop endurance if it's not naturally part of our DNA.

Endurance Is a Formula

So what is endurance?

There is a lot of conversation in modern organizations today about resilience, and Hillary Clinton's quote at the opening of this chapter is representative of the sentiment. Personal resilience is admired and required as the capacity to bounce back when things go wrong or take a different and unexpected direction. Organizational resilience means the same thing, the capability to rise above roadblocks and setbacks. Yet resilience is just one part of the package needed to keep going in today's demanding world. There is more to it than just resilience. It's a formula:

$$Endurance = resilience + adaptability + perseverance$$

The endurance we need for business survival today is a combination of resilience, adaptability, and perseverance. Why? Because business is complex, so to endure—to have the ability to sustain a prolonged stressful effort or activity—is also a more sophisticated concept than just getting your head down and keeping going. It needs some finessing.

Resilience is core to the endurance formula because individuals and organizations do need to be able to bounce back. If we are running marathons, then we need recovery time for our lungs, muscles, and, above all, bones. But it's not enough on its own. We also need adaptability, because new circumstances and different challenges mean that we won't bounce back into exactly the same shape. Our muscles may be stronger and our lung capacity larger, but maybe we have a pulled tendon or shin splints—whatever the differences, our physiology won't be exactly the same, and we need to be able to adapt to our new form. It's the organizations that respond to market pressures and keep developing successfully over time that survive.

And last, we need perseverance. Resilience and adaptability mean that we can bounce back and learn to live in our new form. Perseverance adds the energy to keep us going until we achieve our goals. We need to endure as individuals and as organizations. Let's take a closer look at resilience, the opening part of our formula and start with how to build personal resilience.

Resilience

Resilience is a big topic. If you Google it, you will find more than one resilience institute, most of them with a comprehensive list of indicators. Let's see if we can focus in on a couple of factors that are core in sustaining personal resilience.

Recovery Time and Terror Networks

The danger with running too many marathons is that we don't allow adequate time for rest and recuperation, and so we damage our capacity to cope with the strain. Psychological resilience is an individual's capacity to cope with stress and adversity. A person may suffer from stress and then bounce back, or simply be resistant to stress and not suffer the negative effects at all. Importantly, resilience is a process, not a personality trait. This means that resilience is the result of individuals being able to interact with their environments and have supporting processes that either promote well-being or protect them from the overwhelming influence of risk factors. These supporting processes might be individual coping strategies, or they could be environmental factors like friends or beneficial policies and processes at work.[15] The bottom line is that unnecessary or excessive pressure can put us at risk, and we need coping mechanisms to resist it.

We can learn about recovery time and its importance to resilience in some unlikely places. Think about how terror networks and microbial infections survive despite sustained and powerful attempts to eliminate them.[16] The way they achieve this is by reducing operations to near dormancy for long periods, which gives them the strength to scale up for all-out, periodic attacks. Regrouping and recovery give them the energy for the next assault.

The organizational equivalent that can support employees is to allow time for consolidation. Let's take the example of a CEO who is frustrated by slow progress in executing the strategy and so reaches for another reorganization to create impetus. All the activity may make it feel like we have created momentum, but only if we are sure that we're dealing with the root cause of the problem rather than with a symptom. Reorganizing is the easiest and most visible way to try to induce change, but it's a bit like shaking a cage full of birds. Feathers may be ruffled and the birds may squawk a bit and find different perches, but it's the same old birds and the same old cage. People are adept at making things work despite any inefficiencies in organization design or structure. Rather than more activity, the CEO would be better advised to allow people a period of rest. Consolidation might better enable them to gear up for another push forward in the change program.

It seems a long time since 1984 when the management author and philosopher Charles Handy worried that there would be less work than the expected lifetime 100,000 hours, which had been the norm (47 hours a week, 47 weeks a year, for 47 years).[17] We expected the Internet revolution to increase leisure time and to reduce the amount of paper we use—exactly the opposite has happened. The ease of communication today and the prevalence of global organizations mean that we are even busier and stretched ever tighter. The conference call can happen at any time in a 24-hour period (whether you are the one regularly on the phone in the middle of the night generally depends on how far away you are from headquarters). There is pressure to reply immediately to email whatever time it drops into the inbox. In the United Kingdom alone, 40 percent of workdays are lost because of stress.[18] Something has got to give.

Are We Our Own Worst Enemy?

The bright, gray light of a cloudy summer day streamed in through the wall of floor-to-ceiling windows. The top 100 meeting was in full swing, with the CEO and his Elders in committed attendance. The other three walls were festooned with charts and colored Post-it notes of every shape and size. The aim was synthesis—to reduce the walls of ideas down to five key priorities for the company. It was going to take a lot of talking.

The CEO was grounded and realistic. The only way to make space for five priorities was to spend time also thinking about what they should stop doing, so a whole wall section was devoted to this—what to stop. Some of the list of things to stop was about halting specific business lines or projects—but a great deal more of the list was devoted to reducing "busyness." "Stop e-mail for one day a week; no meeting should last longer than one hour; have better discipline at meetings; reduce the number of conference calls; stop restructuring." One executive spoke up: "We just can't take much more."

The executive team stood at the front of the room and opened the discussion on the list of what to stop—what would be realistic and feasible? The conversation started with the idea of adopting a "no e-mail" policy one day a week. "How about Saturday?" someone jokingly suggested. "I'd prefer Sunday" said another. A ripple of slightly weary laughter ran around the room. It was too close to the truth to be truly amusing. The CEO was genuinely open to the idea of an e-mail-free day a week, but the executives were having none of it. "How can we justify such a delay in responding to our customers?" they chorused. No one wanted a day off e-mail, when it came down to it.

So this question has to be asked: Are we playing some kind of nightmarish global staring game, where no one wants to be the first to blink? In a similar setting, would their customers have said the same? What would their suppliers say? If no one is willing to be the first to stop, we will continue to wind ourselves up tighter and tighter. Instead of feeling pleasantly stretched by the quality of challenging work, we will spring tautly ever upward into the stressosphere.

Or Are We Overtrading on Goodwill?

Chris Argyris, professor emeritus[19] at Harvard Business School, best known for seminal work on "learning organizations," was the first person to coin the phrase "psychological contract" in 1960.[20] It's an important idea. Just as organizations have formal systems (such as pay bands, expense approvals, promotion criteria, procurement rules), they also have informal systems (for example, networks, patterns of influence not dependent upon hierarchy, insider knowledge, gossip). And just as individuals have work contracts, written, explicit, and defined in law, they also have unspoken psychological expectations of their employer, like being safe at work, appropriately consulted, and having some security of employment.

In the 1990s, organizations across the world (less so in some cultures than in others) ruptured the psychological contract with their employees. "Confronted with increased uncertainty, fewer benefits and very often increased workloads and responsibilities, many people feel the psychological contract made between themselves and their organization has been broken."[21] The unwritten expectation of how employees should be treated was unmet or contravened. The primary blow was to the promise of employment. In industry after industry, business after business, organizations' leaders decided that they could no longer promise a job for life. The uncertainties accompanying globalization induced them to offer instead something called "employability." Employment had formerly indicated a job for life. Employability meant a job for as long as the individual's technical and interpersonal skills remained relevant, up to date, and useful.

Life Before We Broke the Psychological Contract

Our newest generation at work, generation Y, sees the new psychological contract of employability as the norm. The Y'ers expect to be trained and offered opportunities, but they are also ready to move on. To the preceding generation of baby boomers (and to some extent gen X workers), it was a dramatic departure from what they had grown to expect. Compare today with previous levels of employer commitment to the physical and emotional welfare of employees. The story of Port Sunlight, which was built by William Hesketh Lever (later Lord Leverhulme) doesn't seem only a century old, more as if it belongs to the Middle Ages. The Port Sunlight development was started in 1888 and represented the Quaker principles of capitalism. (Many modern corporations were founded on Quaker principles, from Amnesty International to Sony. Quakers were trusted to be honest and founded many banks, including Barclays).

The Sunlight development (Sunlight was the name of their most popular cleaning product) was a beautiful garden village of houses built on 56 acres near the River Mersey in England. The houses were built to provide homes for factory workers at the Lever Brothers soap factory (now part of Unilever). There was no expense spared. Lever enjoyed helping to plan the development, and he employed nearly 30 different architects—each house was unique. Port Sunlight also included allotments, a cottage hospital, schools, a concert hall, an open-air swimming pool, a church, and a temperance hotel. He wanted to socialize and Christianize business relations. He looked on it as profit sharing (which wasn't a legal requirement at all), but rather than share profits directly, he invested them in the village. Lever is quoted as saying, "It would not do you much good if you send it down your throats in the form of bottles of whisky, bags of sweets, or fat geese at Christmas. On the other hand, if you leave the money with me, I shall use it to provide for you everything that makes life pleasant—nice houses, comfortable homes, and healthy recreation."[22]

There is no suggestion that we should go back to this model today. What looked like enlightened capitalism at the tail end of Queen Victoria's reign (with no welfare system, people were dependent on the good-heartedness of employers not to exploit them) would now seem like paternalism. But we are even losing more modern attempts to reduce the pressure on individuals. Policies such as closing for business at one set time in the year so that we all take vacation at the same time (taking pressure off, because a lot of e-mail is actually us talking to each other, rather than to customers and suppliers), or insisting that employees shouldn't respond to e-mail while on vacation are also in decline.

We need to ask ourselves the "so what" question—does it really matter? Doesn't every generation change the rules of society and work? Should we just get our heads out of the past and get on with how business runs today?

A Poor Psychological Contract Damages Resilience

It matters because a poor psychological contract damages personal resilience and resilience is an important aspect of endurance. Changing the psychological contract has a detrimental effect on commitment to work, job satisfaction, motivation, and organizational citizenship (the willingness to offer effort altruistically and more than just meet the specifications of the job). And all of these are important factors in building resilience. So, yes, the damage does matter. A good psychological contract makes an employee feel valued and in control. The point here is that every time we change the boundaries of the psychological contract, every time the employing organization offers a little less and expects the employees to offer a little more, it damages individual resilience.

On the other hand, allowing individuals adequate recovery time and providing a steadfast psychological contract at work are central to building and sustaining personal resilience. And it's important. Dean Becker, the CEO of Adaptiv Learning Systems, said, "More than education, more than experience, more than training, a person's level of resilience will determine who succeeds and who fails. That's true in the cancer ward; it's true in the Olympics and it's true in the boardroom."[23]

But we are also part of the problem; if we refuse to ease up on 24/7 communications, we are denying ourselves recuperation time despite any efforts from our employer.

Now let's move on to the second part of the formula, adaptability.

Adaptability

Resilience is vital but insufficient. If the world changes around us and we bounce back, but in the same shape and form, we may be intact but we may no longer be relevant. This is about Darwinism and the need to evolve. How strong and well evolved is your survival instinct? Nothing stays the same. In the volatile and uncertain world of business today, we need to adapt to prosper.

In one sense, we are back to "employability," or keeping ourselves relevant by keeping our skills up to date. We need to be alert to the changing demands placed on the organization because of customer and market evolution or revolution. In Chapter 1, we look hard at the top 100 Village members and stress how critical it is to have their buy-in if the strategy is to stand any chance of being executed. For some of them, this means personal change, letting go of old ideas, and learning new skills to cope with a new world. It's the same throughout the organization. If you are moving from a product-led to a customer-led organization, for example, some of your technical skills will need to be replaced with interpersonal skills. If your company is in transition from being nation-based to becoming international, you will need improved cross-cultural awareness. Don't get stuck in a rut, or you will build in your own obsolescence. While personal change can be hard, your capacity to adapt will ensure your survival and training can help you to keep ahead of the change curve.

What evidence do we have on how good we are at adapting?

How Good Are Leaders at the Tactics of Execution?

Adapting means being able to change and build new skills in response to new demands. There is a host of research that tells us that individual versatility is strongly linked to leadership effectiveness.[24] While part of adaptability is learning new skills, another part of it is making sure that you develop a range of skills and use the right ones, at the right time, at the right level— that is, being versatile. Rob Kaiser, president of Kaiser Leadership

Solutions and senior partner at Kaplan DeVries Inc., has a data-base of information on the leadership versatility of 7,500 managers globally. Of this number, 700 are CEOs or in the top 100 Village. Kaiser measures their versatility on two polarities: how they balance their capacity to push for results against their ability to nurture people and how they balance working strategically against their effectiveness in operations. Good versatility means that the executive does all four well, and Kaiser finds imbalance on the Strategy–Operations polarity. *Strategy* is defined as setting direction, pushing for growth, and supporting innovation. *Operations* means execution, being efficient and focusing resources, and managing with process discipline. Of the 700, only 10 percent turn out to be truly versatile; the other 90 percent overemphasize one or the other side of the equation thus reducing their effectiveness as leaders. And of the 700, two-thirds are judged by their colleagues to focus too little on operations. That is, according to Kaiser's research, two-thirds of CEOs, Elders, and the top 100 Village place too little emphasis on the day-to-day tactical details of implementing strategy. Middle managers score much better on operations.

We don't want to overinterpret Kaiser's findings, but they are interesting. If this is a widespread trend, we'd suggest that our most senior leaders need to pay more attention to developing their effectiveness through improving their focus on operations. Of course, a primary role of senior leadership is in communicating the vision and setting direction, but there is also an important balancing role for senior leaders in ensuring execution. Strategic vision is nothing more than hallucination or mirage if nothing ever comes of it.

Building Adaptability

Adaptability is fundamentally about remaining relevant and effective. There are three stages to building adaptability. The first is to develop self-insight, the second is to address your weaknesses, and the third is to build on your strengths (but not too much).

The self-insight needed here is more than just emotional intelligence, although understanding your personality type and the tendencies you have to approach work in certain ways is one important aspect. It's never too late to start developing self-insight. When Irene Dorner, president and CEO of HSBC America, first started working with her executive team of Elders, she was surprised to find that self-insight was an underexplored capability. "I realized that I had a problem with my top 11 and organized an offsite. They had done no psychometrics and had never functioned as a team, or been told it was important to do so—they didn't know how."[25] Understanding your own tendencies and biases makes it easier to work with others because you can learn to appreciate diversity, rather than be puzzled or offended by different approaches.

But self-insight is also an assessment or an audit of your whole skill base. Look at your technical skills and see if they are current— that is, are they technical skills that your organization still needs today? And what about the future? How far ahead can you look to imagine how your organization will need to change and which skills will become relevant in that future? If you were applying for your own job tomorrow, would you get it? Would you get your boss's job? It's a good idea to get a friend or colleague to help you to take a critical look at yourself. It's not always easy to be as clinical in our self-analysis as we can be about others.

Fix Weaknesses and Build Strengths

The second stage is then to plan to do something about the weaknesses identified in the audit and to decide how to address them. It might be training programs or it might be on-the-job development, like a lateral move or a stretch assignment. Plan to refresh yourself. Sometimes we get so caught up in our own busyness at work that we can drift into irrelevance without even noticing it. Last, look at your strengths and give them a tough audit too. What got you here may not get you there, as the coaching guru

Marshall Goldsmith reminds us in Chapter 2.[26] What was a personal strength at a more junior level of management can be overplayed or not needed to fulfill a more senior executive role. For example, a good grasp of detail could get you promoted into a more senior role while that same strength now comes across as micromanagement, preventing you from spending enough time on strategy. You might still need to understand some of the detail, but you should not focus on it at the expense of the strategic part of your job. And sometimes we hang onto what we know because it makes us comfortable, not because it is necessary.

So far, we have looked at building personal resilience through making space for down time and negotiating a satisfactory psychological contract at work and building adaptability through auditing and upgrading our skill base. Finally, the last part of the endurance equation is perseverance—keeping going until you reach the goal.

Perseverance

J. K. Rowling is famous as the author of the Harry Potter books. She is among the small number of select authors who have become famous and wealthy through their writing. Yet she was rejected by 12 publishers before *Harry Potter and The Philosopher's Stone* was accepted by Bloomsbury and even then apparently at the insistence of the chairman's eight-year-old daughter. Rowling wasn't giving up, and that's what perseverance is all about. Perseverance implies steady persistence toward a goal, despite setbacks or obstacles. Endurance and perseverance combine to win in the end.

Any Color as Long as It's Black

Closer to the business world, Henry Ford is another example of steady perseverance. He was part engineer, part inventor, and part entrepreneur. A talent for engineering and curiosity drove Ford to develop a prototype automobile in his garden. His flair helped him found the Ford Motor Company to develop his prototype. By 1924 Ford had sold 10 million Model T Fords—the car famously available in a choice of colors as long as it was black. During his lifetime his introduction of mass production assembly-line methods irrevocably changed the nature of manufacturing, something for which, for once, the use of the phrase paradigm shift is wholly justified.

Ford was born in 1863 on his father's farm at Greenfield, near Detroit, Michigan. As a boy he showed great interest in mechanics and delighted in dismantling his friends' watches and then reassembling them. The farm was a wonderful playground for engineering development and he built an engine from junk while still a schoolboy. He was always looking for ways to improve things. "Even when I was very young I suspected that much might somehow be done in a better way," he later observed. "That is what took me into mechanics."[27]

After leaving school at 16, Ford went to work as an engineer for James Flower & Co in Detroit. To supplement his meager $2.50 a week, he worked at a jewelers in the evenings. Nine months of grueling hours later, Ford moved to the Dry Dock Engine Works to try his hand at a different type of engineering. By 1896, he was chief engineer at the Edison electric factory in Detroit. His strong work ethic and creative streak kept Ford tinkering with engineering projects at home. His first prototype automobile was the Quadricycle built in his garden shed.

Ford's operational skills appear to have been underdeveloped at this early stage in his career. The Quadricycle was too big to drive out of the shed, forcing him to dismantle part of the shed to release the innovative horseless carriage.

For eight years Ford continued to work 12-hour days and then come home to improve his invention. Yet despite the potential of his automobile, no investor could be persuaded to invest in it. The turning point came when Ford built a car for the Grosse Point automobile races. Although inexperienced, Ford entered the races, drove the car himself, and won emphatically. He repeated the feat the following year, in 1902. The victory attracted financiers and, after a couple of corporate false starts, the Ford Motor Company was up and running. On the way Ford broke the world land speed record for a four-cylinder automobile, driving a mile over the frozen Lake Sinclair in 39 and one-fifth seconds, 7 seconds faster than the existing record.

A lot has been written about Henry Ford, both positive and negative (his management style was widely acknowledged as coercive).[28] On the business side, he transformed what had once been the sole province of the wealthy, the car, into a widely available commodity. Through his perseverance, Ford started an entire industrial revolution of his own founded on his Model T.

KISS

What builds stamina and keeps people persevering? One aspect is certainly being clear about what we are supposed to be doing and not having an overloaded agenda. In Chapter 2 we recommend that the Elders focus on four to five key priorities, on keeping things simple and sharp. Don't overload people or confuse them with too many conflicting messages and priorities. Beware of the danger of initiative fatigue and, as the story earlier in this chapter suggests, keep on top of what needs to stop as well as what needs to start. This has been good advice for over 50 years. Keep it simple stupid or KISS was a design principle started by the U.S. Navy in 1960 and was popular in the 1970s. The acronym was reportedly coined by Kelly Johnson, lead engineer at the Lockheed Skunk Works (creator of the Lockheed U-2 and SR-71 Blackbird spy planes, among many others). Johnson didn't mean that engineers were stupid; just the opposite. The principle is best explained by the story of Johnson handing a team of design engineers a handful of tools, with the challenge that the jet aircraft they were designing must be repairable by an average mechanic in the field under combat conditions with only these tools. Hence, the "stupid" refers to the relationship between the way things break and the (lack of) sophistication of resources available to fix them. So it means that most systems work best if they are kept simple rather than made complex, that simplicity should be a key goal in design and that unnecessary complexity should be avoided. KISS as a strategy execution tool declutters, helping people to be clear about where they are supposed to be heading with a clear focus on what needs to be done to get there.

There are two other pieces to the perseverance jigsaw. In Chapter 3, we talk about meaning at work, so that we are more strongly connected to our goals and motivated by them. Purpose and meaning are not the same. Purpose adds aspiration to our daily work. It gives us the inspiration to commit to stretch targets. Meaning keeps us motivated, with the energy to remain engaged and to keep going—we will persevere if there is meaning to our work. To keep us on the road to our long-term goals, it's about consistency of targets and celebrating short-term task completion or wins. Meaning comes from the psychological closure of seeing a task through to completion; not just any task, but an important task where we can see how it adds to the overall effort of the organization. And then in Chapter 4 we cover connecting through two-way communication so that people are not only clear about what they should be doing, but that they also have the opportunity to offer input and advice and therefore feel a greater sense of ownership of their tasks. In summary, if people are clear about the goal they are pursuing and don't have too many conflicting demands placed on them, they will have focus, hope, and encouragement. They will persevere.

Simplicity and focus, meaning, and knowing that what we do and what we say adds value are the elements that keep us going. We are clear about the end goal, we enjoy the work that will get us there, and we've had a say in what happens.

Short-Termism Again

The greatest enemy of perseverance is the short-term pressure that your organization faces from the market. As a corporation, you are only as good as your last quarter's results. The CEO's duty is to create a sustainable organization, as measured by TSR—total shareholder return. If your shares are not doing as well as those of your competitors, the sound of institutional shareholders stampeding to sell your stock will be deafening. The next quarter's results are immediate and imperative. There is no doubt that you have to devote significant amounts of your attention to the here and now. The challenge facing us all is how to keep persevering for our long-term goals in the face of considerable weight given to the short-term gratification of the market. It's one of the dilemmas that creates the most consternation for executives, and it's a truly challenging problem to solve.

Leaders can have a huge impact on perseverance by role modelling the long term focus that you want to instill in others. Help people develop good habits in energy conservation and building stamina for the journey. Lack of visibility is leaders' biggest sin; you should be in the middle of things, not isolated at the top.

We have now completed the tool kit for individual endurance. It's a combination of resilience, learning how to bounce back; adaptability or keeping upskilled and relevant; and persevering until the long haul of strategy execution, or organizational transformation, is complete.

It's not just individuals who need to develop endurance. Organizations also need to endure to provide long-term prosperity for employees, customers and shareholders. Let's now turn to consider what the same equation looks like for the organization as a whole.

Organizational Endurance

Let's think about the formula for the organization itself. How does resilience + adaptability + perseverance work at this level? Why is it that some organizations, like living organisms, adapt and survive while others do not? How do previously successful organizations drift into irrelevance?

The strategy expert Gary Hamel and Liisa Välikangas wrote an article containing ideas for keeping an organization resilient.[29] Their core thesis was that, "However celebrated, a turn-around is a testament to a company's lack of resilience." They see organizational resilience as continuously anticipating and adjusting to market trends that might permanently damage the core business. There are four steps: (1) to be aware of and acknowledge dramatically changing circumstances (conquer denial); (2) to spread risk through smaller, lower-risk experiments (value variety); (3) to avoid continuing to fund moribund strategies (liberate resources); and (4) to explore new strategic options (embrace paradox). The Hamel model is mostly concerned with being alert and avoiding getting stuck with a strategy past its sell-by date.

This is a good model for creating strategic resilience. However, we need to dig a bit deeper to directly address the challenge of creating organizational resilience, the ability to morph appropriately and quickly. Hamel pleads for a company to have enough strategic insight and verve that it never gets so close to death that the only way out is a wrenching turnaround. Once a crisis looms, people will naturally pull together to survive. That's quite different from creating an organization that can consistently respond to executing a new strategy without missing a beat and with the speed necessary to match the strength of market demand.

The Deification of Leadership

We know that symbolic acts from leaders have a huge effect on us through the subliminal messages they send. If you want people to collaborate, collaborate yourself; if you want people to be customer-focused, visibly spend a good portion of your time with customers yourself; and so on. But it's not enough on its own. As we counsel in Chapter 3, one of the reasons that organizations fail to endure is that they rely too much on the power of charismatic leadership and fail to embed real and lasting change. It's a mistake to overrely on good leadership and altruistic followers to do what is right.[30] We pay attention to how we are assessed and rewarded, as well as to how we are led.

Let's take the classic McKinsey Seven S model, which considers seven internal aspects of any organization that need to be aligned if the organization is to be effective. Leadership is important, but only one of the seven aspects. We can divide the model into two sections.[31] Strategy (being clear about direction), structure (how you are organized to deliver), and systems (the enabling infrastructure, including everything from information technology systems to pay and reward systems) combine to form the "cold triangle." It's called the "cold triangle" because it represents the policies and practices of organization. On the other side, staff (employees), skills (employee capabilities), style (how leaders behave), and superordinate goals (values and culture, or "the way we do things around here") make up the "warm square." It's called the "warm square" because it's all about the people and how they work with and behave toward each other. We need to keep both aspects of the model in sight. If we overrely on leadership, we will fail when poor leaders step in or when strong leaders depart. We need to embed change into the framework and structure of the organization as well, if change is to endure and outlive individual leaders (and employees) as they pass through.

The Cold Triangle

We discuss earlier Hamel's advice on creating a resilient strategy. To create a resilient organization, we need to pay attention to the other two parts of the cold triangle as well—structure and systems. So for organizational endurance, we need to look at issues like systems that really underpin (rather than fight with) the changes we want to make. For example, if the leader advocates collaboration, but employees are rewarded as individuals, then the chances of getting collaboration are severely diminished. So the first argument is for adaptable systems that work with our overall strategic intent. Getting in place consistent systems that work together and talk to each other is a constant challenge in global organizations, which inherit new and often contradictory systems each time they buy a new company to add to the fold. Too often, the plumbing in the company looks more like a Heath Robinson or Rube Goldberg contraption—temporary fixes using ingenuity and whatever is at hand, often string and tape, or unlikely cannibalizations.[32]

Add a Process Perspective

Processes are often seen as the tedious side of organizational life. Leadership is exciting; process is about control. Process relates to activities that are routine, habitual, repetitive, lacking in creativity, devoid of intelligence, uninspiring, and, well, just boring. Worse, adhering to a process implies restriction, constraint, reducing your freedom to act, and stopping you from doing what you want. And process is just a plain bad idea if it means stopping us from exercising our intellect and freedom. But as you exercise your intellectual freedom, so do the rest of your colleagues exercise theirs, each in his or her own endearingly different way. And the result is often chaos. Have you ever found yourself chafing against the inefficiencies in your own business because people are doing their own thing? One of the reasons that McKinsey is so successful is that it takes a strong process approach to its sophisticated advisory work.[33] We need effective processes just as much as we need inspirational leadership.

Good systems and processes (IT, recruitment and reward, procurement, succession planning, development, reengineering, continuous improvement, innovation, and so on) embed endurance. It's like building a house; the very first thing you decide, once the foundations are in and even before the walls go up, is where you want your light switches and plug points. It's hard to do, because it means you have to think in 3D design, and not everyone can do that. You are essentially planning one of the key systems that will underpin and enable the running of the house. Should you be able to build in redundant and back-up systems too, even better.

At home, it means you are never thrust into darkness. At work, they give you a greater chance of being robust against competitive attacks while your company is in transition. Processes that work at cross purposes with strategy execution trip us up and slow us down.

System Interdependencies

Networked businesses build in dependencies on suppliers, joint ventures, and other partnerships. These can work either for or against us, either raising the risk or increasing the available resources. When you start to collaborate with other organizations, it's worth checking out how resilient and adaptable their systems and processes are and also how their systems support long-term thinking. Which assumptions do they factor into their long-term thinking and planning? Interconnected networks increase risk levels and need to be factored into your choice of a partner.

Reaching for the Organization Chart

The third part of the triangle is structure. We argue earlier in this chapter against reaching for the organization chart too quickly to signal that change is necessary. Reorganizations can create unnecessary turmoil and confusion and, if used too frequently, can work against the recovery time we all need if we are to be fit enough to run the execution marathon. The rule of thumb is that "structure follows strategy." Structure is simply an enabling framework. Restructuring can be downright dangerous because people, like animals, fight harder to prevent losses than they do to achieve gains.[34] Any restructuring will create perceived (and actual) winners and losers. The losers will be more active and determined, and, if they are influential, the outcome might be biased in their favor. Under these circumstances, strategic alignment can too easily deteriorate into political coalitions rather than real focus on what must be achieved. At the very least, the restructuring will be more expensive and less effective than it looked in the planning stage—it will create churn, not change. But sometimes restructuring is absolutely necessary as a further enabler to a change process that is already underway. We can't simply rely on leaders. For continuity we need to get the organizational wiring, plumbing, and shape right too. What's the best way to know when it's the right time to restructure?

Form Follows Function

Tony O'Driscoll worked at IBM from 1999 to 2007. His last position was as performance architecture lead, where he led the development of performance analysis techniques to drive sales productivity. Architects say that form follows function, and O'Driscoll agrees. "You need to follow the paths that the new strategy has created and then weave around an organizational structure that works, just before people give up because the old structure starts to get in the way."[35] O'Driscoll is describing the strategic shift that Lou Gerstner (IBM CEO from 1993 to 2002) started in order to move IBM into computing (advisory) and out of computers (manufacturing). Three or four years after IBM sold its computer business to China-based Lenovo in a deal valued at $1.75 billion in late 2004 (retaining only a minority stake in the company), customers were still asking IBM to fix their computers. It takes a while for customers to catch up with big strategic moves that organizations make. Gerstner didn't rush to change the company architecture to match the new business. O'Driscoll recalls, "It felt like the company was still running on its product rails and we were trying to fly an airplane."[36] Working with the old structure in place became increasingly difficult, even though people are ingenious when it comes to getting work done. The upshot was that when the restructuring did arrive, it was welcomed. How often do we hear people groan and complain about yet another unwanted reorganization? Too often. Gerstner managed to reverse that psychology by waiting until employees felt that the structure was getting in their way and then responding to their desire for organizational change.

Back to Baxi

Chapter 4 tells the story of Baxi Heating and the 1990s turnaround that really put employees first and embedded a strong sense of ownership for change on the shop-floor. Author Simon Carter wasn't just after cultural change as human resources director and then CEO. He knew that an enduring focus on customers would need radical structural change as well. It was a Saturday night in October 1989 and Carter was working late at home, long after the family had gone to bed. Pieces of paper representing the different parts of the company structure were spread out on the dining room table. As it got later into the night, he grew increasingly frustrated that he couldn't get the new structure to align. His usually reliable instinct failed to find the breakthrough he was seeking. To add to the frustration, the table he was working on was not quite large enough for all the pieces of paper he needed to display, and some parts of the organization were shunted at awkward angles. Eventually, he grew tired and went to bed, but he was up too early the next day, after a sleepless night.

As he walked downstairs into the dining room, the shape that the paper pieces formed was instantly clear to him. The awkward shape now appeared as circles within circles—an organization with less hierarchy and more support networks spread across it. Each business unit was customer- and service-focused, supported by product and manufacturing teams, all pointing the same way—toward the customers. First he and the Elders had shifted the culture within Baxi. Now it was time to make sure that the organizational structure backed it up and sustained the change. (Fast forward to 2013, and the Cisco organization structure of boards and councils looks remarkably similar and circular.)

To create the enduring organization, we need to do more than update our purpose, what we do, and how we do it. We must address the cold triangle and shift the structure and systems to embed change for the long term—or at least until the next time it changes.

Is There a Denominator?

As with any good formula, there is also a denominator. That is, if the numerator of resilience, adaptability, and perseverance can fight for endurance, however strong these are, there are also elements that can weaken or undermine them. In the case of personal endurance, it's learned helplessness, described in Chapter 4—the moment at which we give up because nothing we do seems to make a difference or enable us to succeed. In the case of organizational endurance, it's a culture of fear, where we are so worried about failure that we avoid risk to the point that it detracts from our ability to set and persevere towards meaningful targets. We need to work to get helplessness and fear out of individuals and out of organizations, or they will undermine all our good work in creating endurance for long-term sustainability.

Summary

This chapter sets out the fifth and final step in our strategy for execution. Unlike strategy formulation, which has become a sprint, we liken strategy execution to a marathon. It takes endurance to move the organization from a CEO announcement to truly embedded change, supported by new systems, processes, and structures, as well as by new working behaviors and a matching set of attitudes. We need to build personal and organizational endurance, which we define as a combination of resilience, adaptability, and perseverance. At the personal level, we recommend building endurance through a combination of a strong psychological contract with our employing organization, as well as through taking recovery time to garner energy, keeping our skills up to date, and focusing on key tasks that give our work lives meaning. At the organizational level, we need to build but then also move beyond good leadership and embed change through supporting systems and organizational structure.

So there we have the complete story. The five steps in the Strategy of Execution are to Mobilize the Village of the most senior executives; make sure they are well led by the executive team as we Gather the Elders; deal with the emotional reactions that all change brings as we Power Up Feeling; Energize People from top to bottom in the organization, so that they truly own strategy execution; and, finally, Build Endurance to run the marathon of strategy execution.

In our final chapter, we offer a self-assessment tool kit so that you can work out for yourself how fit you and your organization are to run the execution marathon.

Thank you for joining us.

6

Five Steps to Strategy Execution

A promise is a cloud; fulfilment is rain.
—Arabian proverb

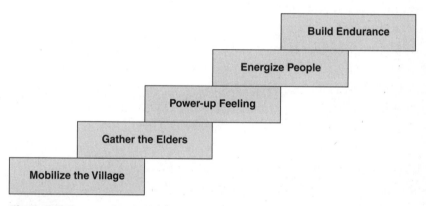

Figure 6-1

Pulling It All Together

We now have our five steps in place, as shown in Figure 6-1, starting on the bottom step with mobilizing the top 100 Village and then climbing them one at a time until we reach the top step, with a sustainable organization set for the long run. Just before the self-assessment, here is a story from one company that illustrates all five steps in action.

BPB plc

British Plaster Board (BPB plc) is a building materials business and is the world's largest manufacturer of plasterboard. The development of plasterboard (a sandwich of gypsum plaster between two sheets of paper) dates back to the late nineteenth century in the United States. An American, Frank Culver, persuaded his new employer, Thomas McGhie and Sons, to buy a plasterboard plant from the United States, which was when this new product was introduced to Britain. Factory construction started in 1916, and in 1917 the plasterboard assets were sold to a new company, British Plaster Board Limited (BPB).

The British building industry was initially slow to adopt the new product. Helped by a more modern plant, purchased in 1927, sales gradually increased, and by 1932 BPB issued stock and was able to float on the London Stock Exchange. By 1990, it was listed in the FTSE 100 index.

In the late 1990s the company embarked on a seven-point business improvement program to increase efficiency and effectiveness, mostly in manufacturing and production. It brought in a world-class manufacturing program for process reengineering and installed a total quality management (TQM) system for lean manufacturing. Through fairly straightforward processes of mechanical and physical change to remove non-value-adding practices, new alignment between supply chain, manufacturing, logistics and distribution delivered business improvements to the bottom line. By 2004, BPB had expanded its global operations through a combination of organic growth and acquisitions to a market capitalization of £4.3 billion, with 12,000 employees and 120 production plants worldwide serving 50 mature and emerging markets.

On a plant-by-plant basis the business had improved, but the then global director of marketing, Gareth Kaminski-Cook, believed that sales and marketing weren't able to deliver sufficient benefits for customers.

Kaminski-Cook knew that to create a world-class capability in sales and marketing, to match what the company had achieved in operations, was going to be tough. Whereas world-class manufacturing had many case examples and benchmarks, there was no such reference point for sales and marketing excellence. Changing manufacturing routines was relatively straightforward as execution dealt with tangible and physical processes. If you improve a process flow of physical work, the benefits are obvious and immediate. Sales and marketing are more about relationships and judgment and would need long-term monitoring to measure qualitative change. Kaminski-Cook developed a strategy for building sales and marketing process excellence, backed by a plan to execute it with a change management program.

The strategy was titled Maximizing Sales and Marketing Excellence but quickly became known internally as MAX. Building upon an existing core of sales and marketing capability, MAX prioritized improvements in four key areas: customer satisfaction, technical sales and solutions, price management, and product/service innovation. We worked alongside Kaminski-Cook from 2004 to 2008.

Mobilize the Village

In 2004 BPB plc was a collection of semiautonomous businesses spread across the globe. There were some corporate policies, but many practices (in all disciplines) were developed locally. To get alignment on one common approach would require careful handling, because not all the managing directors who ran the businesses would be willing partners. They liked their autonomy. But Kaminski-Cook knew that the sales and marketing communities spread around the world hungered for improved standards and discipline. This is where he identified his top 100 Village. The Village members Kaminski-Cook identified were to be the local owners of MAX, the most senior in-country sales or marketing professionals. If he could create momentum, he believed that he could convert the more reticent businesses to adopt new ways of working.

The change process had four stages. The first stage was to evaluate current practices, followed by analyzing the gap between the current state and the desired level of excellence in any or all of the four development areas. There were five levels of excellence, from generalist at the base, rising in competence to specialist, through company expert and industry expert all the way to the fifth and highest ranking of world-class sales and marketing capability. Stage two was to create a development plan. Stage three was to launch the MAX process within prioritized countries, and stage four was a formal review of initial progress in order to lay the foundations for continuous improvement.

Local in-country senior sales and marketing professionals were involved from the start in the gap analysis, so they were well informed about their potential for change and improvement. Their early involvement meant that they also felt ownership of both the problem and the solution to be pursued. The Village was stirring.

BPB was headquartered in the United Kingdom, and the execution process for MAX was planned to roll out in waves of countries over a three-year period. The first eight countries to be involved represented both BPB's best mature markets (United Kingdom, France, Denmark, North America) as well as some of its most challenging emerging and developing markets (South Africa, India, Spain, Poland). There were about 90 Villagers spread across the first eight countries prioritized for the rollout.

Gather the Elders

Each country was led by a managing director (MD). These were the Elders, again spread around the globe. The Elders had sanctioned the exercise in their country but without any real sense of urgency or ownership. It was a "nice to have," not a "must have." They did not become directly involved in the process until the gap analysis and diagnostic report were produced and presented to them. For some, this level of analysis and feedback was unexpected and uncomfortable. It exposed some glaring gaps. The Village, closely involved in the diagnostic, was hungry for improvement and added to the pressure for change.

The MDs of the first eight countries (a group informally referred to as G8), together with the central sales and marketing champions from headquarters, formed an advisory group for the entire execution process. These 11 individuals were the definitive Village Elders. The advisory group was established from the very beginning to champion MAX. Members of the group gave visible business and in-country credibility to the corporate initiative.

Initially, it was difficult to get a real sense of community within this group. The MDs competed with each other, sometimes to an extreme. Each had a natural and strong tendency to want to be seen as the best business performer. The challenge was that, like most Elders, they had the power to make or break the process. The MDs had the most powerful voice. They were given the same training as the local teams, but they were encouraged to lead (not own) the intervention. It was time-demanding, and some of the Elders were initially resistant to support what they saw as an unproven and time-consuming project. Proof of success would come only from results after the rollout, and for some that leap of faith was a jump too far. The doubters were inclined to withhold support, fail to commit to actions, or move very slowly. In contrast, those who bought in started to show real passion for the change and visibly championed it. Game on.

Kaminski-Cook kept his nerve and kept pushing gently, but firmly. Some Elders struggled to provide the full breadth of leadership needed, and failure in some countries was directly related to the MD's inability to lead. This had to be tackled head-on. In one country, the program was stopped by the MAX team until the executives would commit properly. Some heavyweight Elders began to express public doubts about the alleged benefits, and the change teetered on the edge of being undermined. Timing is everything. Luckily, early successes from the countries that embraced the change built confidence that Kaminski-Cook was able to leverage. These leaders needed to be credible and believable, not just at the launch, but through the entire program of change. It turned out that some Elders were naturally effective communicators but that some needed help to get the messages across. As confidence in the change grew, they were willing to accept the help they needed to make it work.

Power Up Feeling

MAX was 20 percent process change and 80 percent attitude change. Kaminski-Cook's team had built a framework so that for the first time countries could be assessed on a comparable platform. The five levels of achievement, from generalist all the way up to world class, brought discipline to measurement and instilled a real sense of ambition to aspire to a higher level of performance.

After the diagnostic and gap analysis had been digested by the country management teams, the training started. The launch event in each country brought the entire local sales and marketing teams together and was designed to be challenging and inspiring. For some countries, just getting everyone together was novel. The launch day was supported by headquarters' sales and marketing champions for each of the four elements of the change initiative. It was delivered by them working alongside the local sales and marketing teams.

This was the time to get buy-in from a broader audience and was a key event. The launch content was designed to build reassurance and also deal with emotional challenges and resistance to change. Training built new skills and confidence. (Sales and marketing are hardwired to be good at understanding individual psychology and emotion, because this is what drives buyer behavior.) It was also intended to build excitement; for example, the South African launch was led by a Zulu dance. At the German launch, a rather stiff opening presentation was livened up by the trainer standing close behind the presenter, inserting his arms through the presenter's (which were clenched to his sides), and making exaggerated hand signals. A certain amount of irreverence loosened people up and made the event memorable—it signaled that the path ahead was intended to be fun as well as transformational.

Energize People

After the launch, local teams started to work on performance improvement. Each team set a change agenda built around the four improvement areas. The sequencing of change was determined by the gap analysis and agreed upon with the headquarters' champion. Each team set goals in six or seven key areas and developed projects and action plans to deliver them. These projects importantly included every function, because a journey toward being more market-driven was a culture change for BPB. It would affect every function, and messages needed to be communicated up, down, and across every channel. The projects focused tightly on the four improvement areas so that BPB could keep on track to achieve stronger customer focus.

A culture of execution is about communications, ownership, and follow-through. Communications and ownership were built through the diagnostic phase, launch, and subsequent one-day face-to-face events. A MAX magazine was launched with news snippets and updates. Follow-through came via a centrally run global audit process. There was a drumbeat of regular virtual checks on progress with the local teams, and momentum and pace were deliberately tight. There were also more formal face-to-face, one-day reviews, at which PowerPoint presentations were banned. Teams had to build storyboards describing the process, attitude, and behavioral changes they had delivered. At the close of the review day, the headquarters' champion and the local team agreed on enhanced performance targets, and the cycle was set to repeat at six-month intervals. Each review also had time allocated for learning more about change management and a slot for a one-on-one review between the headquarters' MAX champion and the MD. The one-day events were action packed, empowering, and creative. There was excitement in the air.

In time, stories of excellence and achievement began to emerge. After a year, the headquarters' champions began to build cross-country networks and hubs of local expertise. These developed into communities of excellence, and the people in them met every year—at the Tump—to share best practices and over time to refine the structure and architecture of the whole MAX program. The cogs multiplied and gained momentum and velocity.

Build Endurance

Over three years, the program was eventually rolled out to 24 countries. The headquarters' MAX champions worked a punishing schedule of launches, audits, and excellence workshops. Because countries were clustered into groups of six or seven, it was not unusual for these champions to visit four or five countries on consecutive days to deliver the program. From London to Bangkok, Kuala Lumpur, Shanghai, and a final stop in Mumbai was a typical five-day run. Each country was on an 18-month cycle, and the agenda became complicated as well as stretching once 24 countries were involved, all at different stages in the cycle. The champions needed huge reserves of stamina to see it through, and new ones were recruited over time.

It had been clear from the start that the difference between the successful and less successful applications was the attitude and conviction of the local leader, the MD. Elders make a difference, and where they lacked adaptability, progress slowed. Kaminski-Cook and his team just kept going. They didn't allow setbacks to distract them and recognized that these were radical changes which would necessitate substantial behavioral change for some countries. Kaminski-Cook's team members' perseverance and resilience built their credibility and believability, which in turn created confidence in the local teams, which then built increased buy-in from the local MD. It was a virtuous circle.

MAX evolved over time. The communities of excellence allowed core processes to flex to meet local conditions without compromising the core principles. Above all, the headquarters and local champions kept adapting over time to update and reframe targets as they passed key milestones. The waves of launches built into an unstoppable tsunami of change.

BPB regained its place in the FTSE 100 Index in June 2005 after an absence of 14 years. The company accepted a bid from Saint-Gobain that valued the company at £3.9 billion. BPB was delisted in December 2005. Saint-Gobain kept MAX going, and by 2007, more than €30 million in financial gains had been identified from actions taken.

This Is What It Takes

This is the reality of successful strategy execution. It takes time, energy, effort, and focus. It's systemic. You can't swallow a magic pill or pull one or two levers and it's all done. That's why we lay it out in five steps. It's not always easy, but, if you persevere to the end, it's enormously satisfying. Achieving successful change enables the long-term sustainability of the organization and guarantees employment. Not achieving change brings confusion and churn and an overload of "initiative-itis," as you try to kick-start the failed change process again. We cannot underestimate the effort it takes to keep delivering short-term targets for the current strategy at the same time as gearing up to deliver on the new strategy. Creating a new strategy is glamorous work, but the real heroes and heroines of organizations are those who execute with efficacy and conviction.

The five steps of strategy execution are steep and sequential. It is difficult—if not impossible—to advance successfully by trying to jump over steps. All are important. Our five steps are intended to give you confidence as well as being a practical framework from which to build your own execution agenda and process. As much as strategies are planned as coherent, logical, and sequential activities, the practice of execution is not linear but messy, dynamic, and emergent.

In today's interconnected and immediacy-driven business world, we have seemingly lost our tolerance for things taking time. There may be a slow food movement, but there is not a business equivalent. We are rotated onto the next job before we have had time to see the results from the existing job, so we don't have the chance to follow through or measure the impact. We are seduced by the flattery of being in demand, so with Blackberry always in hand, busyness takes over and stops us from taking the time to connect with others so that they feel and own the execution of strategy. Because we feel driven, our empathy dissipates, and we become impatient for others to move at warp speed alongside us. Our own behavior acts as a poor role model for the communication, ownership, and follow-through that underpins a culture of execution.

Strategy execution takes time.

Trying to move too fast routinely fails because of a lack of ownership, direction, traction, and belief. As you look around, how nimble, flexible, and adaptable is your organization and what is its state of readiness for change? What momentum can you generate to drive progress at the appropriate speed to ensure that tipping points are reached without tipping over? Building momentum is a judgment call. Move too fast and you risk failing to get real ownership, and you dangerously overbuild your confidence through mistaking the behavior of others as commitment when it's actually compliance. Move too slowly and the coalitions of resisting forces will dig in and build their networks of infection.

Finally, a thought about your leadership. We believe that most people show up at work every day ready to do a good job. Most are followers, and execution is all they experience—it's the daily reality of their working lives. They don't have the privilege of leading strategy execution. As a leader, how they feel about their daily work of execution is derived from how you make them feel. They will inspect the logic of your argument as they seek to make sense of the strategy. But above all, they will test your believability and work out whether you can be trusted to lead them somewhere new and different.

How good are you?

Self-Assessment Guide

Mobilize the Village

1. Have you identified your top 100 Village? (Who are the Villagers, and how many of them are there?)
2. Are the right people in the Village? (How did they get there? Are they the real power brokers in strategy execution?)
3. Does the Village meet face to face at least twice a year for four days at a time?
4. Does the Village have a sense of identity and community?
5. What are you doing to bond the Village members into a more visible and unified community?
6. How do you encourage individual members to align through community-oriented behaviors, and how do you measure them against these?
7. Can they articulate the strategy clearly for others, with energy, knowledge, and conviction?
8. Do they own the strategy execution agenda, and how are you developing the Villagers to take real ownership?
9. Do you have the courage to confront and move the wrong people out?
10. How do the members of the Village relate to the Elders (are they well led)?

Gather the Elders

1. Who are your Elders (more than just the executive team working alongside the CEO, not all of the executive team, some influential others)?
2. Are they clear on what type of strategy you are pursuing (chronic illness, chronic wellness, surgery, or trauma)?
3. Has the CEO challenged or evicted Elders who don't understand or agree with the strategy?

4. Are the Elders showing the right kind of leadership to match the type of strategy being pursued (are they credible and believable)?

5. Do your Elders collaborate well? (If they play Politics with a capital "P," have they been challenged to play nicely together?)

6. Have the Elders agreed with the CEO on the four or five unequivocal and clear strategic imperatives for the organization to replace, not be added to, earlier imperatives?

7. Is the Elders' emotional intelligence as well developed and deployed as their intellect?

8. Do your Elders lead strategy execution, rather than trying to own or execute it themselves (is the Village motivated to be led by them)?

9. Are the Elders talking about what really matters in "red flag" conversations, to reach true agreement on the strategy and how to execute it?

10. Do the Elders implement good practices for efficient and effective governance and an appropriately demanding drumbeat for execution?

Power Up Feeling

1. Do you make decisions largely based on rationality and evidence (do you sometimes get stuck in analysis paralysis)?

2. Do you understand the role that emotion and instinct play in decision making (can you trust your instinct and guard against bias)?

3. Are the consultants you hire creative enough and do they speak your business language (or do they expect you to speak theirs)?

4. Do you understand the emotional stages people go through when faced with change?

5. Can you demonstrate the right behaviors to support others through the emotional phases of change (metaphorical hugs, listening, being influenced in order to be more influential)?

6. If you are ahead on the change curve, can you control your reactions and impatience while you wait for others to catch up?

7. Can you connect with others so that you can consistently and frequently make the case for change through understanding what they hope to get from it?

8. Do you truly live the changes that you want to see from others (do you give them confidence)?

9. Does your organization have purpose as well as vision (and can you tell the difference between the two)?

10. Does your work and the work of others have meaning (identify with the job, it feels important, can see tangible results, and know how I am doing)?

Energize People

1. Have you identified all the different villages in your organization that need to meet in conversation at the Tump in order to move strategy execution forward together (and have you clarified that they all have equal value)?

2. Do you understand that a culture for execution is a combination of communication, ownership, and follow-through?

3. Instead of communicate, communicate, communicate, do you know how to connect, connect, connect?

4. When was the last time you were trained in effective conversation skills and storytelling?

5. Do you feel ownership of the strategy, or do you feel helpless as its execution advances toward and over you (do you know what power you really have)?

6. Do you work in a culture of fear (or can people share their views honestly and without fear of retribution)?

7. Can you learn from failure as well as from success?

8. Are people really regarded as the greatest asset in your organization (and how do they come first)?

9. Is there a performance orientation in your organization (do managers understand, own, and use the performance management system for real)?
10. Do people follow through on goals and measure achievements, not activity?

Build Endurance

1. Have you put in the training for the strategy execution marathon (are you physically and mentally strong, reached elite status on key skills, confident, can you beat boredom)?
2. Do you chunk it up and celebrate milestone targets so that you keep running until the finish line?
3. Did you know that endurance is a combination of resilience, adaptability, and perseverance?
4. Are you resilient (how well do you bounce back from adversity)?
5. Do you allow yourself adequate rest and recuperation time?
6. Have you built a solid, trusting, and mutually beneficial psychological contract with your organization?
7. Are you adaptable (are your skills and capabilities up to date and relevant to today's business challenges)?
8. Can you persevere diligently until milestones are met and execution is complete (can you resist the pressure in the short term in order to keep going for the long term)?
9. Do you have the endurance and patience to run the strategy execution marathon (or one marathon after another)?
10. How enduring is your organization itself (do you have good systems and structures supporting your endeavors as well as strong leadership of them)?

How did you do?
Good luck!

Notes

Introduction

1. Plunkett Research Ltd., plunkettresearch.com, see "Introduction to the Consulting Industry."
2. Joseph Isern and Caroline Pung, "Organizing for Successful Change Management: A McKinsey Global Survey," *McKinsey Quarterly*, June 2006.
3. John P. Kotter et al., *HBR's 10 Must Reads on Change Management* (Cambridge, MA: Harvard Business Press Books, 2011).
4. Yang Li, Sun Guohui, and Martin J. Eppler, "Making Strategy Work: A Literature Review on the Factors Influencing Strategy Implementation," ICA Working Paper 2, Business School, Central University of Finance and Economics, Beijing, China and Institute of Corporate Communication, University of Lugano (USI), Lugano, Switzerland.

Chapter 1

1. Sam Walton was Walmart's founder. Walmart was back at the number one spot in the Fortune 500 company ranking in 2013.
2. The World Economic Forum is a Geneva-based nonprofit foundation. Every year it conducts a meeting in Davos, Switzerland, which brings together top business leaders, international political leaders, selected intellectuals, and journalists to discuss the most pressing issues facing the world.
3. Ben Worthen, "Cisco CEO John Chambers' Big Management Experiment," August 5, 2009, http://blogs.wsj.com.
4. Ellen McGirt, "How Cisco's CEO John Chambers Is Turning the Tech Giant Socialist," *Fast Company,* December-January 2009.
5. Author interview with Dominique Fournier.

6. George A. Miller, "The Magical Number Seven, Plus or Minus Two: Some Limits on Our Capacity for Processing Information," *Psychological Review*, vol. 63, no. 2, 1956, pp. 81–97. This article, by a cognitive psychologist at Princeton University, is one of the most highly cited papers in psychology. It is often interpreted to argue that the number of objects an average human can hold in working memory is 7 ± 2. This is frequently referred to as *Miller's Law*. The world moves faster today because of technology-led hyperconnectivity. We think that five is the new magical number, replacing seven.

7. D. Nelson, *Frederick W. Taylor and the Rise of Scientific Management* (Madison, WI, University of Wisconsin Press, 1980).

8. David Jackson and John Humble, "Middle Managers: New Purpose, New Directions," *Journal of Management Development*, vol. 13, no. 3, 1994, pp. 15–21.

9. "Thawing Out GM's Frozen Middle," *Business Management Daily*, July 4, 2013.

10. Tom Peters, *Liberation Management: Necessary Disorganization for the Nanosecond Nineties* (New York: Alfred Knopf, 1992).

11. "Middle Managers; Saving David Brent," *The Economist*, August 15, 2011. The David Brent reference concerns the popular TV series, *The Office*, where middle managers such as the Brent character played by Ricky Gervais are self-obsessed and incompetent.

12. Marcus Buckingham and Curt Coffman, *First Break All the Rules: What the World's Greatest Managers Do Differently* (New York: Simon and Schuster, 1999).

13. Wayne F. Cascio, "Downsizing: What Do We Know? What Have We Learned?" *Academy of Management Perspectives*, vol. 7, no. 1, February 1, 1993, pp. 95–104.

14. Joe Ryan, "Caught in the Middle: Why Developing and Retaining Middle Managers Can Be So Challenging," Knowledge@Wharton, May 28, 2008.

15. You could argue that it should be a hamlet, but this is a U.K. construct (in which a *hamlet* becomes a *village* when it gains the right to build its own church), while *village* has this meaning in many cultures.

16. Roger I. M. Dunbar, "Neocortex Size as a Constraint on Group Size in Primates," *Journal of Human Evolution*, vol. 22, no. 6, June 1992, pp. 469–493.

17. We'd never heard of them either. The Hutterites are a communal branch of Anabaptists who, like the Amish and Mennonites, trace

their roots back to the Radical Reformation of the sixteenth century. The Hutterites believe in shared community life and pacifism.

18. Interview of Richard Branson by Jason Ankeny, *Entrepreneur*, June 19, 2012.

19. "The World's Biggest Public Companies," *Forbes*, Forbes Global 2000 list, www.forbes.com/global2000.

20. "Sir John Bond Lays Bare HSBC's Strategy for Gaining Ground," *Thebanker.com*, June 10, 2003.

21. Justin Sullivan, "HSBC Ends US Subprime Lending," *Boston Globe*, March 3, 2009. "It's an acquisition we wish we hadn't done with the benefit of hindsight, and there are lessons to be learned."

22. Author interview of Irene Dorner. Note that Dorner uses the term *elevator* to refer to a crisp summary of any message that can be easily understood in a short amount of time.

23. James C. Collins, *Good to Great: Why Some Companies Make the Leap . . . and Others Don't* (London: Random House U.K., 2001).

24. Author interview with David Levin.

25. Nothing grows in permafrost. Overlaying it may be a thin active layer that thaws seasonally in the summer. Plant life can be supported only within the active layer, as growth can occur only in soil that is fully thawed for at least some part of the year.

26. John Hagel and John Seely Brown, "Harrah's New Twist on Prediction Markets," Businessweek.com, Innovation and Design, December 22, 2008.

27. "The World's Biggest Public Companies, *Forbes*, Forbes Global 2000 list.

28. Author interview with Tom Albanese.

29. Ibid.

30. In *Uncle Tom's Cabin, or Life Among the Lowly* (1852), Harriet Beecher Stowe describes the character Topsy as a wild and uncivilized slave girl whom Miss Ophelia tries to reform. In Chapter 20, in a conversation between Ophelia and Topsy, the girl, who never knew her mother and father, decides that nobody made her—"she just *grow'd*."

31. Albert Hirschman, *Exit, Voice, and Loyalty: Responses to Decline in Firms, Organizations, and States* (Cambridge, MA: Harvard University Press, 1970). Research in the context of consumer loyalty.

32. Author interview with Karina Robinson.

33. Ibid.

34. Author interview with Nick Forster.

35. Ibid.

36. An advocate is someone who believes in the same things that you do, who supports you and can persuade others to follow. Beware of "hot advocates" who understand the "new world" fast and then surge ahead, trying to make it happen. They tend to scare people away. See Liz Mellon, *Inside the Leader's Mind—Five Ways to Think Like a Leader* (Upper Saddle River, NJ: Prentice Hall, 2011).

37. Author interview with Irene Dorner. Stephen Bungay talks about something similar, although less visual, in his book *The Art of Action* (London, UK: Nicholas Brealey Publishing, 2011).

38. Dennis Hevesi, "Colin Marshall Dies at 78; Helped Turn Around British Airways," *New York Times*, July 13, 2012, p. B10.

39. Author interview of a former CEO who requested anonymity.

40. The term *air cover* refers to aircraft used to protect and otherwise support ground troops.

41. Steve Kerr, the American academic who was central to building GE's famous training university at Crotonville, NY, wrote the article, "On The Folly of Rewarding A While Hoping for B," *Academy of Management Journal*, 1975, pp. 769–783.

Chapter 2

1. Yves Doz and Mikko Kosonen, "The Dynamics of Strategic Agility: Nokia's Rollercoaster Experience," *California Management Review*, 2008.

2. Dave Lee, "Nokia: The Rise and Fall of a Mobile Giant," BBC News, Technology, September 3, 2013.

3. Markku Ruottinen, "Nokia CEO Stephen Elop Admits Failure to Foresee Sector Changes," *Aamulehti* (Finnish national daily), June 28, 2012.

4. Dave Lee, "Nokia: The Rise and Fall of a Mobile Giant," BBC News, Technology, September 3, 2013.

5. Nic Fildes, "Finland's Finest Concedes Defeat and Hands Itself to Microsoft for €5bn," *The Times*, September 4, 2013.

6. Stephen Elop, "Full Text: Nokia CEO Stephen Elop's 'Burning Platform' Memo," *TechEurope*, blog edited by Ben Rooney, with contributions from *The Wall Street Journal* and Dow Jones Newswires, February 9, 2011.

7. Author interview with an anonymous Villager.

8. J. E. Rosenbaum, "Tournament Mobility: Career Patterns in a Corporation," *Administrative Science Quarterly*, vol. 24, no. 2, pp. 220–241.

9. Scott DeCarlo, "The World's Biggest Companies," *Forbes,* April 18, 2012.

10. Tuomo Peltonen, "Facing the Ranking from the Past: Tournament Perspective on Repatriate Mobility," *International Journal of Human Resource Management,* vol. 8, no. 1, 1997, pp. 106–123.

11. Arthur Jensen, *Straight Talk About Mental Tests* (New York: Free Press, 1981).

12. Daniel Goleman, *Emotional Intelligence: Why It Can Matter More Than IQ* (London: Bloomsbury, 1996).

13. Author interview with Sir Jeremy Greenstock.

14. Marshall Goldsmith, *What Got You Here Won't Get You There* (New York: Hyperion, 2007).

15. Warren G. Bennis and James O'Toole, "Don't Hire the Wrong CEO," *Harvard Business Review*, May 1, 2000.

16. J. B. Leslie and E. Van Velsor, *A Look at Derailment Today: North America and Europe* (Greensboro, NC: Center for Creative Leadership, 1996).

17. John P. Kotter, *Leading Change* (Cambridge, MA: Harvard Business School Press, 1996).

18. Author interview with Jeremy Pelczer.

19. Of course, we have to be worried about dysfunctional teams as well, with poor practices like groupthink, where each team member adopts the overall team view myopically, even though the team view is flawed. For more on this and similar topics, read Patrick Lencioni, *The Five Dysfunctions of a Team* (San Francisco: Jossey-Bass, 2002).

20. Author interview with David Levin.

21. The Growth-Share Matrix is a chart created by Bruce Henderson for the Boston Consulting Group in 1970 to help corporations analyze their business units or product lines. "Stars" are businesses with the highest future growth potential according to this matrix, and firms are advised to invest in them.

22. You can take the consultants out of a business school, we confess it's harder to take the business school out of the consultants. We fall too easily into the trap of the classic 2 × 2 matrix used by all business schools and tend to see them everywhere—so we couldn't let David Levin have a three-pronged model.

23. Eugene J. McCarthy, James J. Kilpatrick, and Jeff MacNelly, *A Political Bestiary: Viable Alternatives, Impressive Mandates, and Other Fables,* (New York: McGraw-Hill, 1978).

24. Ruth Alexander, "Which Is the World's Biggest Employer?" *BBC News Magazine*, March 20, 2012.

25. Author interview with Jeremy Pelczer.

26. Author interview with Tony O'Driscoll. (Armonk, in the town of North Castle, NY, is IBM's headquarters in the United States.)

27. Louis V. Gerstner, Jr., *Who Says Elephants Can't Dance?: Inside IBM's Historic Turnaround* (New York: HarperCollins, 2002).

28. Professor Cliff Bowman of Cranfield University coined the term "ZOUD," an acronym for "the zone of uncomfortable debate." Cliff Bowman, "Strategy Workshops and Top-Team Commitment to Strategic Change," *Journal of Managerial Psychology*, vol. 10, no. 8, 1995, pp. 4–12.

29. The earliest citation for "red flag" in the *Oxford English Dictionary* is from 1602; it shows that at that time the flag was used by military forces to indicate that they were preparing for battle.

30. The Time-Turner is a fictional device capable of time travel that looks like an hourglass on a necklace. The academically gifted character Hermione Granger was given one by Professor McGonagall in J. K. Rowling's book, *Harry Potter and the Prisoner of Azkaban* (New York: Scholastic, 1999), so that she could attend two classes at the same time.

31. Stolen from *Star Trek*, where the prime directive is that there should be no interference with the internal development of alien civilizations.

Chapter 3

1. Pramod Bhasin was the president and CEO of Genpact, a spinoff of GE, which he founded in 1997 while still employed there. He is currently non-executive vice chairman of Genpact.

2. The expression "black swan" comes from a Latin expression "*rara avis in terris nigroque simillima cygno*" ("a rare bird in the lands, very much like a black swan"). In English, when the phrase was coined, the black swan was presumed not to exist. Black swan events were introduced by Nassim Nicholas Taleb in his 2001 book *Fooled By Randomness*, to denote unexpected events with large consequences, such as the advent of the personal computer.

3. Nigel Nicholson, *Executive Instinct* (New York: Random House/Crown, 2000).

4. Daniel Kahneman, *Thinking, Fast and Slow*. (London: Allen Lane, 2011).

5. Author interview with Jeremy Pelczer.
6. Antoine Bechara, Hanna Damasio, Antonio R. Damasio, and Gregory P. Lee, "Different Contributions of the Human Amygdala and Ventromedial Prefrontal Cortex to Decision-Making, *Journal of Neuroscience*, July 1, 1999.
7. Anita Roddick, *Body and Soul: How to Succeed in Business and Change the World*, autobiography (London: Random House/Vermilion/Ebury, 1992).
8. Author interview with David Levin.
9. Wikipedia to the rescue. The claim that there are "many Eskimo words for snow" is a widespread, though disputed, idea that Eskimos have an unusually large number of words for *snow*. In fact, the Eskimo–Aleut languages have about the same number of distinct word roots referring to snow as English does, but the structure of these languages tends to allow more variety as to how those roots can be modified in forming a single word.
10. Hans Christian Andersen, "The Emperor's New Clothes," 1837. A short tale about two weavers who promise an emperor a new suit of clothes that is invisible to those unfit for their positions, stupid, or incompetent. When the emperor parades before his subjects, a child cries out, "But he isn't wearing anything at all!" The moral decries vanity.
11. This phrase was coined by Tom Peters in 1978 when he was consulting with McKinsey. He met the president of Hewlett-Packard, John Young, who described it to him as one of Hewlett-Packard's secrets. Peters is still a great fan of this approach today.
12. Author interview with Nick Forster.
13. Daniel Goleman, *Emotional Intelligence* (London: Bloomsbury Publishing, 1995).
14. *Star Trek* fans compile lists of scenes in which the usually logical Mr. Spock is surprisingly emotional.
15. Author interview with anonymous female senior executive with AstraZenica and GlaxoSmithKline.
16. With apologies to Dan Ariely for using the title of his book, but it just works here.
17. The Kübler-Ross model, commonly referred to as the *five stages of grief*, is a hypothesis introduced by Elisabeth Kübler-Ross in her 1969 book *On Death and Dying*, which was inspired by her work with terminally ill patients. Kübler-Ross's hypothesis was that when a person (and/or the survivors) is faced with the reality

of impending death, he or she will experience a series of emotional stages: denial; anger; bargaining; depression; and acceptance (in no specific sequence). This model has been extended and expanded by later writers and broadened to refer to loss more widely.

18. Herbert Dwight Kelleher is the charismatic former CEO of Southwest Airlines, who was famous for bear-hugging employees to demonstrate his gratitude for their hard work.

19. A. D. Wolvin and C. G. Coakley, *Listening, Understanding, and Misunderstanding* (New Orleans: Sage Publications, 1996).

20. Author interview with Ali Gill.

21. Y. Doz and M. Kosonen, *Fast Strategy: How Strategic Agility Will Help You to Stay Ahead of the Game* (Harlow, UK: Pearson Education, 2008), Chapter 9, "Energizing Hearts," pp. 167–182.

22. Gary Yukl and John W. Michelin, "Proactive Influence Tactics and Leader Member Exchange," in C. A. Schriesheim and L. L. Neider, eds., *Power and Influence in Organizations: New Empirical and Theoretical Perspectives* (Greenwich, CT: Information Age Publishing, 2006), pp. 87–103.

23. Professor Rob Goffee, London Business School.

24. More precisely, Mahatma Gandhi said, "Be the change that you wish to see in the world."

25. Albert Mehabrian, *Silent Messages,* (Belmont, CA: Wadsworth, 1971). A classic study that is often misquoted as, "the total impact of a message is based on: 7 percent words used; 38 percent tone of voice, volume, rate of speech, vocal pitch; 55 percent facial expressions, hand gestures, postures and other forms of body language." This is the 7 percent–38 percent–55 percent rule. But Mehabrian never claimed that you could view a movie in a foreign language and guess 93 percent of the content by watching body language. His research was focused on the communication of emotions—specifically, liking and disliking. The nonverbal aspect of communication *won't* deliver 93 percent of your entire message, but it will reveal underlying emotions, motives, feelings, and, particularly, any dissonance between what you say and how you sound and look.

26. Arthur Brisbane, "Speakers Give Sound Advice," *Syracuse Post Standard*, March 28, 1911, p. 18.

27. *Fortune* editors, "IBM's Ginni Rometty on Leadership," transcript, October 2, 2012.

28. Charles Handy, *The Hungry Spirit* (London, U.K.: Hutchinson, 1997).

29. Jay A Conger, *Winning 'Em Over: A New Model for Management in the Age of Persuasion* (New York: Simon & Schuster, 1998).

30. For example, Lawrence G. Hrebiniak's comprehensive book *Making Strategy Work: Leading Effective Execution and Change* (Philadelphia: Wharton School Publishing/Pearson Education, 2005) talks about people first in Chapter 7, and his strategy execution model doesn't include people at all.

31. The term *cognitive dissonance* was coined by Leon Festinger in his 1956 book *When Prophecy Fails* (Minneapolis, MN: University of Minnesota Press) to describe the followers of a UFO cult as reality clashed with their fervent belief in an impending apocalypse. Festinger subsequently (1957) published another book called *A Theory of Cognitive Dissonance* (Stanford, CA: Stanford University Press) in which he outlines the theory. Cognitive dissonance is one of the most influential and extensively studied theories in social psychology.

32. Emily Lawson and Colin Price, *The Psychology of Change Management* (London: McKinsey, 2003).

33. Maslow's hierarchy of needs is a theory in psychology proposed by Abraham Maslow in his 1943 paper, "A Theory of Human Motivation." Maslow used the terms *physiological, safety, belongingness, love, esteem, self-actualization,* and *self-transcendence needs* to describe the pattern that human motivations generally move through.

34. J. R. Hackman and G. R. Oldham, "Motivation Through the Design of Work: Test of a Theory, *Organizational Behavior and Human Performance*, vol. 16, no. 2, 1976, pp. 250–279.

35. Teresa Amabile and Steven Kramer, *The Progress Principle: Using Small Wins to Ignite Joy, Engagement and Creativity at Work* (Cambridge, MA: Harvard Business Review Press, August 2011).

36. Teresa Amabile and Steven Kramer, "How Leaders Kill Meaning at Work," *Harvard Business Review*, January 2012.

Chapter 4

1. Arthur Jensen, *Straight Talk About Mental Tests* (New York: Free Press, 1981). The average executive IQ is 125 multiplied by the 35 executives in the room = 4,375 IQ points.

2. Gary L. Neilson, Karla L. Martin, and Elizabeth Powers, "The Secrets to Successful Strategy Execution," *Harvard Business Review*, June 2008. Also, Arthur A. Thompson, Jr., Margaret Peteraf, John E.

Gamble, and A. J. Strickland, *Crafting and Executing Strategy: The Quest for Competitive Advantage: Concepts and Cases* (New York: McGraw-Hill, 2011).

3. Peter F. Drucker (1909–2005) was an Austrian-born U.S. management consultant, educator, and author, whose writings contributed to the philosophical and practical foundations of the modern business corporation. He was also a leader in the development of management education, and he invented the practice of management by objectives. Look at Brainy Quotes (online) for a list of his wonderful thoughts.

4. Author interview with Jeremy Pelczer.

5. Stephen Bungay in his book *The Art of Action* (London: Nicholas Brealey Publishing, 2011) adopts the armed forces' term *backbriefing* to describe this process.

6. Author interview with Irene Dorner.

7. Jerome Bruner, "Actual Minds, Possible Worlds," the Jerusalem-Harvard lectures, Harvard College 1986. Also LeanIn.Org video by Stanford Professor Jennifer Aaker.

8. Michael Beer et al., *Managing Human Assets* (New York: Free Press, 1984) suggested that "truth must speak to power."

9. Brainy Quote.

10. Michael Beer, *High Commitment High Performance: How to Build a Resilient Organization for Sustained Advantage* (San Francisco, CA: Jossey-Bass, 2009).

11. Professor Gary Latham, Rotman School of Management, University of Toronto, Canada.

12. Henry Ford, the founder of the Ford Motor Company, is attributed as saying, "Why is it every time I ask for a pair of hands, they come with a brain attached?"

13. One of Anita Roddick's favorite quotations displayed on the side of Body Shop trucks.

14. Grant Thornton reported in the January 2013 *UK Business Confidence Monitor* that businesses were still cautious about investing in the recovery, as highlighted by continued low capital investment and salary growth. In March 2013, the Ifo Institute in Munich, Germany, said its business climate index, based on a survey of 7,000 executives, showed a decline in German business confidence. There are many other similar indexes of business confidence.

15. Author interview with Nick Forster.

16. Carol Dweck, *Mindset: The New Psychology of Success* (New York: Random House, 2006).

17. Author interview with Nick Forster.
18. Carol Dweck, *Mindset: The New Psychology of Success* (New York: Random House, 2006).
19. *The Proverbs And Epigrams of John Heywood*, 1562. Yes, we thought it was from *Alice's Adventures in Wonderland* by Lewis Carroll too.
20. Author interview with Dominique Fournier.
21. Japan is still suffering from the recession that started in 1989–1990, when the bubble of high land prices burst; see *BBC Business*, August 14, 2002, and the *New York Times*, February 13, 2013, for examples of commentary on this subject.
22. Nicholas Carr, *The Shallows: What the Internet Is Doing to Our Brains* (New York: W. W. Norton & Co., 2010).
23. Marcus Buckingham and Curt Coffman, *First Break All the Rules; What the World's Greatest Managers Do Differently* (London: Simon and Schuster UK, 2005).
24. Author interview with Jeremy Pelczer.
25. Edwin A Locke, "Toward a Theory of Task Motivation and Incentives," *Organizational Behavior and Human Performance*, vol. 3, 1968, pp. 157–189. Also see Edwin A. Locke and Gary P. Latham, *A Theory of Goal Setting and Task Performance* (Englewood Cliffs, NJ: Prentice Hall, 1990).
26. This is not a reference to a Justin Bieber song but is intended to mean "never give up."

Chapter 5

1. Interview with Sir Jeremy Greenstock, former U.K. ambassador to the United Nations.
2. The University of California at Berkeley Haas School of Business Dean's Speaker Series featured John Chambers, Tuesday September 28, 2010 at 12:45 p.m. in the Andersen Auditorium.
3. Author interview with Tom Albanese.
4. Stefan Stern, "Feel the Strategy: Leaders Must Exchange Hearts as Well as Minds," *Management Today*, November 1, 2008.
5. The marathon guidelines are drawn from a variety of sources, including interview material from Chuck Engle, who has won 148 marathons, average finish time 2:44, including wins in 50 U.S. states, as well as author Liz Mellon's experience as a marathon runner.
6. Author interview with Ali Gill.

7. Meyer Friedman, *Type A Behavior: Its Diagnosis and Treatment* (New York, Plenum Press/Kluwer Academic Press, 1996).

8. Connie J. G. Gersick, "Time and Transition in Work Teams: Toward a New Model of Group Development," *Academy of Management Journal*, vol. 31, no. 1, 1988, pp. 9–41.

9. Form = the group assembles; storm = there is initial debate and disagreement on how the work should be carried out; norm = the group agrees on standard working procedures, which it adopts and keeps throughout the execution of the task; perform = only once the group has agreed its process can it move to effective task achievement.

10. Jim Collins told a similar story about Walgreens' exit from the restaurant business in "Level Five Leadership: the Triumph of Humility and Fierce Resolve," *Harvard Business Review*, January 2001.

11. After several decades of empirical study, Elliott Jaques (a Canadian psychoanalyst and organizational psychologist) concluded that humans differ in our ability to handle time-dependent complexity. We all have a natural time horizon we are comfortable with, what Jaques called, "Time span of discretion," or the length of the longest task an individual can successfully undertake. Jaques observed that organizations implicitly recognize this fact in everything from titles to salary: line workers are paid hourly, managers receive bonuses annually, and senior executives are compensated with longer-term incentives such as stock options. His research is regarded as controversial today. For example, see Elliott Jaques, *Requisite Organization: A Total System for Effective Managerial Organization and Managerial Leadership for the 21st Century* (Arlington, VA: Cason Hall & Co., 1989, 1996, 1998).

12. Charles Darwin, Chapter 14, "Concluding Remarks and Summary," in Charles Darwin, *The Expression of the Emotions in Man and Animals* (New York: D. Appleton and Company, 1872), pp. 347–366.

13. Melinda Wenner, "Smile! It Could Make You Happier," *Scientific American*, October 14, 2009.

14. Tara Kraft and Sarah Pressman, "Grin and Bear It: The Influence of Manipulated Positive Facial Expression on the Stress Response," *Psychological Science*, August-September 2012.

15. B. Leadbeater, D. Dodgen, and A. Solarz, "The Resilience Revolution: A Paradigm Shift for Research and Policy," in R. D. Peters, B. Leadbeater, and R. J. McMahon, eds., *Resilience in Children, Families, and Communities: Linking Context to Practice and Policy* (New York: Kluwer, 2005), pp. 47–63.

16. A. Zolli and A. M. Healy, *Resilience* (London: Headline Publishing Group, 2012).

17. Charles Handy, *The Future of Work* (Oxford, UK: Blackwell Publishers, 1984).

18. The HSE Annual Statistics Report for 2011–2012 showed that, in the United Kingdom alone, over 27 million working days were lost, with 10.4 million of these being the result of stress. Separate research carried out by Friends Life released in November 2012 found that 32 percent of the working population in the United Kingdom have taken a day off work because of stress.

19. The emeritus title is bestowed on professors who are so famous that their employing institution never wants them to retire. Professor Argyris was 90 in 2013.

20. Chris P. Argyris, *Understanding Organizational Behavior* (Homewood IL: Dorsey Press, 1960). Edgar H. Schein further expounded on the subject: *Organizational Psychology* (Englewood Cliffs, NJ: Prentice Hall, 1980).

21. J. M. Hiltrop, "Managing the Changing Psychological Contract," *Employee Relations*, vol. 18, no. 1, pp. 36–50.

22. Quoting from *William Hesketh Lever: Port Sunlight and Port Fishlight,* (London: Development Trust Association, 2007. Probably better is the biography by Adam MacQueen, *The King of Sunlight: How William Lever Cleaned Up the World.* (Ealing, UK: Bantam Press/Transworld, 2004).

23. Dean Becker quote on Adaptiv Learning Systems' website.

24. Bob Kaplan and Rob Kaiser, *The Versatile Leader* (San Francisco: Pfeiffer Wiley, 2006).

25. Author interview with Irene Dorner.

26. Marshall Goldsmith, *What Got You Here Won't Get You There: How Successful People Become Even More Successful* (New York: Hyperion Books, 2007).

27. Henry Ford autobiography, *My Life and Work*, by Henry Ford, in collaboration with Samuel Crowther (Garden City, NY: Doubleday, Page & Co., 1923).

28. Anne Jardim, *The First Henry Ford: A Study in Personality and Business Leadership* (Cambridge, MA: MIT Press, 1970).

29. G. Hamel and L. Välikangas, "The Quest for Resilience," *Harvard Business Review*, September 2003.

30. D. L. Bradford and A. R. Cohen, *Power Up: Transforming Organizations Through Shared Leadership* (New York: John Wiley & Sons,

1998). The authors argue for postheroic leadership that is more inclusive of others.

31. The McKinsey 7S Framework is a management model developed by well-known business consultants Robert H. Waterman, Jr., and Tom Peters (who also authored *In Search of Excellence* in the 1980s).

32. William Heath Robinson (1872–1944) was the English cartoonist and illustrator best known for drawings of eccentric machines. In the United Kingdom, the name "Heath Robinson" has entered the language as a description of any unnecessarily complex and implausible contraption, similar to "Rube Goldberg" in the United States, who is best known for a series of popular cartoons depicting complex gadgets that perform simple tasks in indirect, convoluted ways.

33. Liz Mellon, David C. Nagel, Robert Lippert, and Nigel Slack, *The New CFOs: How Finance Teams and Their Leaders Can Revolutionize Modern Business* (London: Kogan Page, 2012).

34. Daniel Kahneman, *Thinking, Fast and Slow* (New York: Farrar, Straus & Giroux, 2011).

35. Author interview with Tony O'Driscoll.

36. Ibid.

Index

About the Authors

Dr. Liz Mellon has spent the last 25 years designing, developing, and delivering leadership development programs, initially as a professor at London Business School and currently as executive director at Duke CE, the world's leading executive education provider. The world's most influential global ranking of management thought leaders, Thinkers50 has listed Mellon on its "Guru Radar."

Simon Carter, former CEO of Baxi Heating UK, was featured by the BBC for his work in leading corporate transformation during a period of challenging union dominance in the 1990s. Since stepping down as chairman, Carter has been an advisor to FTSE companies all over the world.